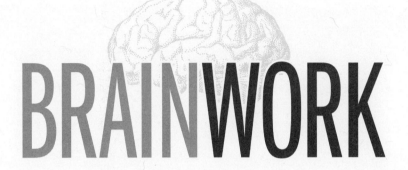

BRAINWORK

The
Neuroscience
Behind How
We Lead Others

DAVID A. *Sousa*

TRIPLE
NICKEL
PRESS

555 North Morton Street
Bloomington, IN 47404
888.369.3179
FAX: 888.467.5986

email: info@triplenickelpress.com
triplenickelpress.com

Printed in the United States of America

16 15 14 13 12   1 2 3 4 5

Library of Congress Control Number: 2011944485

ISBN 978-0-9833020-3-2
eISBN 978-0-9833020-4-9

President and Publisher: Robert D. Clouse
Vice President of Production: Gretchen Knapp
Managing Production Editor: Caroline Wise
Senior Production Editor: Lesley Bolton
Proofreader: Elisabeth Abrams
Text and Cover Designer: Jenn Taylor

Table of Contents

Introduction

The brain is a wonderful organ: It starts
working the moment you get up in
the morning and does not stop until
you get into the office.

ROBERT FROST

A s THIS BOOK WENT TO PRESS, AMAZON'S WEBSITE LISTED MORE THAN 36,000 books that have some connection to the brain. You can find books on how your brain grows and develops, what makes it happy or sad, how to keep it healthy, how it makes decisions, and how it can get you into trouble. There is definitely no dearth of information about the human brain, especially since the advent of imaging technology several decades ago. Brain books are in vogue. But with so much information available, where do you start? *Brainwork* compiles and condenses this information, throwing out the half-truths and addressing common myths to provide you with the must-have information regarding the brain's inner processes and their applications to the workplace.

If you consider yourself a multitasker or believe the old shibboleth that "knowledge is power," you're in for a few surprises. Some of the new revelations in brain research run counter to long-held beliefs in organizational management. Gone are the days of "it's not personal; it's just business." Today's business world requires a closer look at emotional intelligence, and the best decision makers use both their emotional brains and rational brains. Multitasking is no longer considered a coveted trait but rather a hindrance to productivity. In fact, multitasking as we know it doesn't even really exist. And what happened to morality and ethical behavior? Have they gone the way of the dodo?

In the upcoming pages, we'll take a closer look at these subjects and explore ways to improve your thinking, control stress in the workplace, and lead by dissent. Of course, brain health is most important, so we've devoted a chapter to taking care of your brain, including what type of diet, what amount of exercise, and how much sleep are needed to maintain a healthy brain, especially as we grow older. Findings from brain research are suggesting strategies that can expand your existing cognitive networks and build new ones—in other words, make you smarter and more creative! Read on and find out how.

CHAPTER ONE

The Curse of Too Much Information

Everybody gets so much information all day long that they lose their common sense.

GERTRUDE STEIN

A T THE VERY MOMENT I REALIZED I HAD TO BUY A NEW CAR, A COLD CHILL came over me. I had flashbacks to a similar event eight years earlier (I keep my automobiles for a while) that turned into unpleasant haggling and tiring drama. Frankly, entering a dentist's office for a root canal is less disturbing to me than entering a new-car showroom.

I was cheered by the thought that my decision on the car's make and model would be easier this time, given all the information one can find on the Internet about new cars. And so my hunt began. First, I compared ten models on the car manufacturers' sites, including trunk size, gas mileage, and dozens of options—fancy ones, such as seat warming and cooling, and not-so-fancy ones, such as GPS location technology and side air bags. Already the number of possible permutations of models and options was becoming enormous. Next, I looked at several dozen written and video reviews from people who already owned the cars. Regrettably, some reviews praised model A but trashed model B, whereas others did the reverse. Then I collected several reports and recommendations from consumer advocate organizations. Add to this already dazzling amount of information the need to make a decision on whether to purchase or lease, along with evaluating the dealers' special offers, such as cash-back incentives and low financing rates. In just a few days, I had so many facts, figures, and opinions that my head was spinning. To make matters worse, the results of all this effort were inconclusive.

In the end, I visited several car dealers and eventually bought the car I liked. Damn the data, I decided to go with what looked and felt like the right choice! After more than a year, I can honestly report that I am very happy with my selection.

This experience, no doubt, occurs thousands of times a month. Prospective car buyers make conscientious attempts at due diligence by investigating various makes, models, options, and reviews. Some people carefully assess the available information and make a quick, conscious choice based primarily on the data they have collected. But for many others, despite what the data reveal, they often end up delaying their decision and eventually buying the car that pleases them, the one that feels right. These buyers most likely base their decision on what some call a "gut reaction," one that overrides—but doesn't necessarily contradict—the data. They experience a deeper form of mental processing that involves unconscious thought and emotions.

But does this approach cause buyers to later regret their decision? Apparently not. Studies, like those carried out by psychologist Ap Dijksterhuis of Radboud University in the Netherlands, have shown that buyers who waited and mulled over the information for a while were more pleased with their eventual purchase than those who made a purchase immediately after reviewing the data.[1] This was true whether they purchased a car or a house. Likewise, Claude Messner and his colleagues at the University of Basel in Switzerland recently found that information overload decreased consumer satisfaction in their choices, and reducing the amount of information increased unconscious thought and choice satisfaction.[2]

The results of these studies seem counterintuitive. Surely, the more information we have, the better our decisions. Or not? Could this notion, which has been the mainstay of management courses for decades, be flawed? What's going on here? To explain how unconscious thought and feelings can be so powerful and often make the right choice, we need to understand some basic facts about how our brains deal with incoming information.

The Brain Does Not Treat All Information the Same

The human brain evolved over many years through three basic stages (see fig. 1.1). The oldest part is the brainstem, sometimes called the reptilian brain because it resembles the entire brain of a reptile. This vital area controls and monitors functions necessary for our survival, such as breathing, body temperature, heartbeat, and digestion. Any

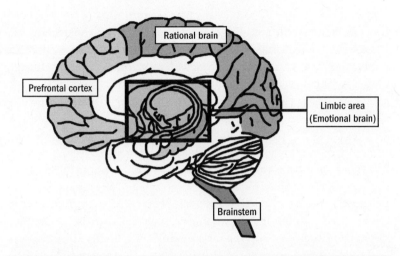

Figure 1.1: The three major parts of the brain and the prefrontal cortex.

incoming information that can affect our survival, such as a snarling dog or a burning odor, gets highest priority for processing. Survival information comes first.

Just above the brainstem is the next oldest area, known as the *limbic system*, responsible for processing emotional information and generating emotional responses. This area is often referred to as the *emotional brain*. Because emotions play an important role in maintaining family and community bonds, as well as in securing a mate, outside stimuli that contain emotional information have the next highest priority.

Finally, the last and largest area of the brain to develop (and thus the newest) is the *cortex*, or the *rational brain*. It makes up about 85 percent of the human brain's weight. Most reasoning occurs in the forward part of this region, called the *prefrontal cortex*, located just behind the forehead. The prefrontal cortex is responsible for solving problems, making decisions, and controlling emotions. Any incoming cognitive information not vital to survival or wrapped in strong emotion ends up here.

Whenever we respond emotionally to a situation, the limbic system plays a major role. Sometimes the emotional response is so intense that the more rational cognitive processes are suppressed or suspended. We have all experienced situations in which joy, anger, or fear of the unknown overcame our rational thoughts. Such a scene may result in us losing our ability to move ("I froze") or to speak ("I was dumbfounded"). Alternatively, it can lead us to do or say something that we regret later on when our rational brain perks up and remarks, "I can't believe you did that!" So how do the information-processing hierarchy and the touchy relationship between our rational and emotional brains explain why consumers who based their choice on feelings were more satisfied with their final selection than those who relied mainly on information? Did emotions take over and the rational brain toss all that information aside? Not exactly.

The Limited Capacity of Working Memory

Psychologists have known for a long time that our short-term memory (now called *working memory*), located in the prefrontal cortex, has a limited capacity. Back in the 1950s, George Miller from Princeton University's psychology department suggested that the maximum number of items an individual could hold in working memory was seven, plus or minus two.[3] (Perhaps that limit explains classic heptads, such as the seven deadly sins, seven seas, seven wonders of the world, and seven-digit telephone numbers.) However, recent research by Michael Kane (University of North Carolina, Greensboro), Randall Engle (Georgia Institute of Technology), and others suggests that this number is overstated and that our current capacity is closer to three to four items.[4] Nonetheless, when working memory capacity is reached, something has to happen.

Get a pencil and a piece of paper. Stare at the number below for seven seconds, then look away and write it down. Ready? Go.

3521904

Compare the number you wrote down to the number above. Chances are high that you got it right. Now, let's try that again, using another number and the same rules. Stare at the number below for seven seconds, look away, and write it down.

9237546302

Check what you wrote down. How did you do this time? Chances are you left out some digits. That's because your brain treated each digit as a separate item, so your working memory got overloaded and simply ran out of capacity. This can also happen when you include too many variables when making an important business or personal decision. Items can slip out of working memory and not be considered as part of the decision at all. And this might be a good thing.

Dijksterhuis' studies found that when people were faced with purchasing decisions involving just a few variables, they took time to
mull over the options before deciding and were satisfied with their
choice.[5] For those who made impulsive decisions, regret set in as they
soon realized they didn't really want or like what they bought. The
results changed considerably when the purchasing decision involved
a large number of variables—for instance, buying furniture or a new
car. Working memory could not focus on so much information and
often chose to focus on just one variable, such as color or size. The
end result was that the longer people analyzed their choices, the less
satisfied they were with their purchasing decisions. Who were the
most satisfied? Those who didn't spend much time thinking about all
the information and just let their emotional brain make the selection.

Researchers in this area are not suggesting that the emotional brain
entirely co-opts the decision-making process when working memory
is overloaded. Rather, they suggest that just a few salient facts and
feelings are processed over time below the level of consciousness—in
unconscious thought—while the individual is engaged in unrelated
conscious activities. Eventually, this unconscious process renders a
decision that we recall and act on.

Exactly what happens in the brain during working memory overload has been the interest of researcher Angelika Dimoka at Temple
University's Center for Neural Decision Making.[6] She has studied the
effects of too much information by working with bidders who are
involved in a complex marketing frenzy called combinatorial auctions.
These are bidding wars for numerous items that people can buy alone
or bundled, such as landing slots at a busy metropolitan airport. The
vast number of variables that the bidders need to consider eventually
leads to information overload. Dimoka used a brain imaging technique known as functional magnetic resonance imaging (fMRI) to measure
brain activity in the prefrontal cortex.

As the bidders received more and more information, Dimoka noticed
that activity in the prefrontal cortex decreased quickly (see fig. 1.2,
page 8). Working memory was getting full and rebelling. The bidders
began to make dumb mistakes and bad choices because the prefrontal
cortex essentially abandoned its role as the reasoned decision maker.
Furthermore, without the prefrontal cortex exerting its control over
the limbic system, emotions began to run rampant, causing a rise in

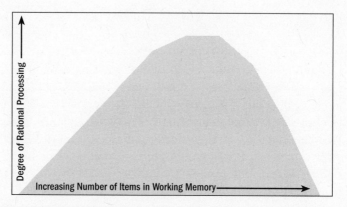

Figure 1.2: Rational processing increases as the number of items in working memory increases. However, after working memory capacity is reached, adding more items of information causes a sharp decline in rational processing, resulting in poor decisions.

the bidders' anxiety and frustration. This combined effect resulted in many bad decisions or no decision at all. Apparently, if a little knowledge is a dangerous thing, too much knowledge can be paralyzing.

One curious characteristic of working memory is the way it assigns importance to incoming information. In any learning situation, we tend to remember items presented at the beginning and the end much better than the items that came in the middle. The opening and closing of a presentation stay with us longer than the material in between. Researchers call this the *primacy-recency effect*. You probably experienced this effect earlier when you tried to remember that ten-digit number. Chances are high that you remembered the first several digits (9, 2, 3, 7) and last several (3, 0, 2) but had difficulty remembering those in the middle (5, 4, 6).

Figure 1.3 illustrates how the degree of remembering varies throughout a learning situation. At the beginning, working memory has the capacity to process new information, so it commands our attention (the first peak in the figure). However, as the number of new items approaches the capacity limit, anything else coming into working memory is likely to be lost or remembered only partially (the dip in the figure). As the presentation concludes, working memory sorts the information and once again pays attention, this time to the final items (the second peak).

Because of this effect, we are likely to give more importance to the most recent information we receive, while giving little weight to what

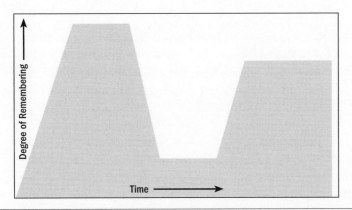

Figure 1.3: How much we remember in a learning situation depends largely on when it is presented. We remember the first and last items best.

came earlier. In this day, when information arrives often and fast, we frequently mistake immediacy for quality.

Too Much Information or Too Little Attention?

Every instant, the human brain does an enormous amount of information processing as signals race across neurons to keep our minds alert and our bodies alive. Some experts claim that there are as many as a quadrillion (1,000,000,000,000,000) instructions zooming around the brain every second. Granted, many of these signals are handling *internal* information, such as body temperature, blood pressure, heart rate, movement, and other such functional data. But even if this estimate is only partially close to reality, why does such processing power prevent us from coping with *external* information overload? Actually, the problem is not processing capacity so much as it is attention span.

As we noted earlier, working memory has a limited capacity. The human brain tries to focus on a small number of items to determine whether they should be stored or rejected. As more items enter the system, attention shifts among them and focus diminishes. In effect, we lose our ability to concentrate on single items long enough to determine their importance. Items blur into a vague mass of unknown importance, and the brain responds with frustration and anxiety.

British marketing analyst Gary Giddings offers a simple mathematical expression for this phenomenon.[7] He says that the amount of total attention available (A) is equal to the number of items in an information source (s) multiplied by the amount of attention needed to examine each item (a). Thus, $A = a \times s$. Let's take a closer look at the import of this expression. Total attention available, or A, can be both a constant and a variable. At work, we subconsciously set the attention span time for items based on our previous experiences handling similar problems and by estimating how much time we can devote to the task before something else comes along. As a result, most people have a fairly constant attention span (A) when dealing with information at work. Consequently, if A is constant, then as the number of information items (s) increases, the amount of time spent on each (a) has to decrease. Giddings wisely avoids putting numbers into his equation, because the attention resources and allocations are not that precise.

The total attention available, however, can vary dramatically when the situation changes. For example, the time we are able to attend to a task may be much longer when we are dealing with information related to home activities, such as interacting with a spouse or children, or when involved in a hobby. When I was a superintendent of schools, I often had to struggle to concentrate for just a few minutes on what seemed to be a silly problem that someone should have solved at a lower level. (I had lots of these on some days.) Yet, I could go home that same day and spend hours concentrating on an article about new discoveries in brain research. My attention span increased when the situation changed to something of greater interest to me. This example also explains why most of us are apt to respond to the ring of a cell phone even though we are trying to complete a work-related project. *Oh, who could that be? How important is it?* Interest perks up, and some of the attention resources devoted to the work project are diverted to musing about—and perhaps answering—the phone call. We might justify this action by saying that we are simply multitasking, but as we shall see in the next chapter, that explanation just doesn't cut it.

Too Much Information May Not Be Good for Your Health

You know the drill. You want to get some information for a presentation you are giving to the senior vice presidents. As part of your presentation, you want to show your competitors' sales numbers from the last quarter. You decide to search the Internet or an online database: *Hmm, which of the 200,000 sites should I search? Which of the 150 press reports on these companies should I read? Oh, great! There are conflicting sales data from different sources. Which ones should I trust?*

Information overload is described as the feeling you get when being inundated by too much information at too fast a pace to use it appropriately. It is often associated with a sense of being overwhelmed and a loss of control. It is not a new phenomenon. In the Bible we find, "Of making many books there is no end; and much study is a weariness of the flesh."[8] The eighteenth-century French author Voltaire noted, "The multitude of books is making us ignorant." Only a few decades ago, the major sources of information were radio, television, printed media, and phone calls. Today, we have technologies, such as the Internet, personal digital assistants, computers, smartphones, iPads, and iPods, that allow us to send and receive music, videos, text messages, instant messages, and digital attachments, as well as set up our own social media pages, blogs, and websites.

A few people have the remarkable ability to scan and process enormous amounts of information quickly and accurately—but they are very few and far between. It doesn't always mean that those people will make a good or even a timely decision. I once had a boss who insisted on amassing copious data and analyzing every possible aspect of a problem and the potential solutions, no matter how trivial the problem. He would write each chunk of data, option, and possible consequence on separate index cards and shuffle them around a table in his office like a battlefield commander planning an invasion. By the time he made a decision, either the problem had resolved itself or no one cared about it anymore.

Most of us have much smaller processing limits, and when those limits are reached, anxiety begins to build. This anxiety is described as *perceived information overload*, and it may not be good for your health. Researchers Shalini Misra and Daniel Stokols of the University of California, Irvine worked with nearly 500 college students to determine how they responded to perceived information overload.[9] The students were to consider two sources of information over a six-week period: cyber-based and place-based. The cyber-based sources were those in which information flowed through the Internet and portable technologies. Place-based sources were those that did not involve electronic technologies but came instead from social interactions in physical settings at home, in the workplace, or in the community. These sources also included environmental pollution, noise, crowding, and commuting and traffic congestion.

At the beginning of the study, the participants completed questionnaires about their perceived information overload, perceived stress, health status, activities for contemplation and reflection, and their sensation-seeking levels. This last category was studied to test the notion of whether high sensation seekers would be more resistant to stress than low sensation seekers. Participants answered questions about their general health and identified any stressful life events (such as separation or divorce, illness, personal injury, or death of a family member) that occurred during the previous year. The survey on perceived information overload from cyber-based sources asked the participants if they: (1) were frequently overwhelmed with electronic messages and phone calls, (2) had too many instant messages, as well as Facebook and MySpace messages, (3) were pressured to respond quickly to such messages, (4) were spending too much time attending to their technology, and (5) received more messages than they could handle. Questions regarding place-based sources of information asked whether they (1) felt hassled by their commute to and from work, (2) were bothered by noisy work or home environments, (3) were overwhelmed by the demands of their workplace, and (4) had too little time for rest and recreational activities.

Six weeks later, the participants completed surveys on their perceived stress and overall health. For example, they were asked how often they had health problems in the previous three months and to identify specific symptoms they experienced during that time period, such as headaches, feelings of depression, acid indigestion, and insomnia. Participants who said they had high levels of cyber-based overload in the initial surveys reported in the follow-up surveys that they had higher levels of stress and more frequent and severe health problems. Curiously, the place-based information overload had no discernable impact on stress, but it did have a negative effect on health.

This study had some other interesting findings that executives may wish to ponder. First, individuals who said they were high sensation seekers reported lower levels of stress from cyber-based overload compared to those who said they were low sensation seekers. Second, participants experiencing high levels of cyber-based information overload said they had little time for contemplative and reflective activities. When working memory is crammed with information, there is little room left for self-reflection and for contemplating the consequences of pending decisions.

A survey of business managers in Britain reported by David Bawden of the Department of Information Science at the City University London had some surprising revelations.[10] Two-thirds of these managers believed information overload had caused a loss of job satisfaction and damaged their personal relationships. About one-third believed it had damaged their health, and nearly half believed important decisions were delayed and adversely affected because of having too much information.

Bawden and his colleague Lyn Robinson later went on to describe several forms of strange behaviors that arise when people are faced with overwhelming amounts of information.[11] Particularly amusing is the term *infobesity*, a sort of feasting excessively on information as though it were fast food. Treatments for this condition include *information avoidance*, which is essentially ignoring relevant and useful information because there is too much of it, and *information withdrawal*, which is keeping the number of information sources to a minimum.

Then there is *satisficing*, a coping strategy whereby one takes in just enough information to meet a specific need and ignores the rest. This could be considered a practical approach for one who is not aware of the full range of choices. Simply glean the information that is good enough and do not worry if the best information is unavailable. Many new-car buyers resort to satisficing rather than dealing with the dizzying amount of data on car models. They pick two or three possibilities based on their experience or a friend's recommendation, and then they seek out some basic information about each: Is the gas mileage reasonable? How well does it survive crash tests? How does it look and feel behind the wheel? And that's it!

Psychologist Barry Schwartz of Swarthmore College argues that the bewildering variety of choices available in modern life (think not only car models, but the different kinds of cereals, jams, and blue jeans) causes anxiety and has paralyzing effects on our ability to make choices.[12] To him, satisficing is a valid approach because it lowers stress and increases happiness. Although satisficing may be useful when making choices in the supermarket or department store, it may not be an appropriate method for making executive decisions in a business. There are risks to this seemingly sensible option. More effective choices may be overlooked, and the process may be reduced to information avoidance, a potential calamity in the marketing world. To prevent this, there should be a clear rationale to support any decisions made through satisficing.

The Impact of Information Overload on Decision Making

Scientific research on how we make decisions continually undermines the old notion that the more information we have about a situation, the better. As more information bombards us more often and more incessantly, we are discovering that it has detrimental effects on rational processing, problem solving, and decision making. Let's take a look at what can happen.

Making No Decision

Not long ago, I visited a neighbor who had just bought a fifty-inch flat-screen television with an astounding array of features. The clarity and resolution of the picture were very impressive, and the multiple speakers enveloped me in bone-rattling sound. I was enthralled with this technology because my current television is a twelve-year-old, twenty-seven-inch set with a picture tube (remember those?) and two small front-facing speakers. It occurred to me that a set this old was probably going to fail soon—the perfect excuse to visit a local branch of a national electronics store. After fifteen minutes of roaming around the cavernous place, I found the multiple aisles of television sets. Counting brand names, models, picture sizes, and other options, there were more than 120 different choices. The variety was beyond my expectations, and the data paralyzed my thought processes. Fortunately, a rescue was imminent.

The television sales assistant approached and offered his help. He asked what kind of television set I currently owned and was surprised that it had the old-fashioned picture tube. Before I could say, "I'm just looking," he proceeded to describe all the models and options. He made his preferences clear, explaining the technical data that proved how sensible his choices were for me. "Which one would you like to take home?" he asked. Overwhelmed by the choices, I thanked him and walked hurriedly out of the store. I pray that my old set will provide a few more years of service before I have to face that scene again.

Numerous studies show that when people are dealing with too much information and have too many choices, they are likely to make no decision at all. For example, Sheena Iyengar, a professor of business at Columbia University, and her colleagues have done a number of "too many choices" studies.[13] One of these looked at the participation rate of employees in voluntary 401(k) plans offered by the Vanguard investment group. The investment executives were puzzled as to why there was such low participation, given the wide variety of plans that employees could choose from.

The researchers looked at the records of about 800,000 employees in more than 600 different companies. They discovered that as the number of plan options increased, participation in the plans decreased. When there were just two options, 75 percent of eligible employees participated, but when the number of options rose to fifty-nine, participation dropped to 61 percent. The many choices were so overwhelming that 14 percent of participants dropped out, and nearly 40 percent of employees opted not to enroll in any plan. They just could not make a decision. This result was bewildering because the nonparticipating employees not only were sidestepping the opportunity to establish a retirement nest egg, but were also passing up a gift from their employers, many of whom matched employee retirement contributions up to a set amount. At the same time, the employers who thought they were improving the financial well-being of their workers by offering more retirement plans were actually causing enrollment in these plans to drop. A positive goal but a negative outcome.

Even a seemingly simple decision, like buying a jar of jam, can be bewildering if the amount of information is excessive. In a California supermarket, Iyengar and colleague Mark Lepper set up a jam-tasting booth that switched each day between offering an assortment of six jams or twenty-four jams.[14] These were just a small sampling of the brain-numbing 348 varieties available in the jam aisle of the store. Shoppers who stopped by the booth were able to sample each jam and receive a coupon that would take one dollar off every jar of jam they bought.

Not surprisingly, only 40 percent of incoming shoppers stopped at the booth when the researchers displayed just six jams, but that jumped to 60 percent when they displayed twenty-four jams. Obviously, the larger assortment appealed more to shoppers than the smaller one. However, when the time came to select a jam from the jam aisle, the shoppers who had seen only six jams had a much easier time deciding which jam to purchase. Listening in on the shoppers' conversations in the jam aisle, the researchers discovered that the small assortment helped the shoppers to narrow down their choices, whereas the large assortment left shoppers confused and uncertain about their own preferences. In the end, the shoppers who stopped by the smaller assortment bought six times as much jam as those who stopped by the larger display, even though the latter was more popular. Too many varieties led many to a decision not to buy.

In another study, marketing experts Maria Sicilia and Salvador Ruiz of the University of Murcia in Spain created three versions of a website, each with increasing amounts of information about items available for online purchase.[15] As potential buyers scrolled through the site that had the most product information, they felt overwhelmed and their thoughts drifted away from their purchasing task, resulting in disinterest. More importantly, they made few or no purchases.

Making a Poor Decision

No matter how experienced you are, too much information can derail your decision-making process. This is not a new discovery. As far back as the late 1980s, Paul Andreassen at MIT conducted an experiment with a group of business students who were to buy and sell stocks in an imaginary portfolio.[16] Each student selected a portfolio of stocks. Andreassen then divided the students into two groups. The first group had access to all the financial information they desired. They read financial newspapers, watched financial broadcasts on television, and were able to contact stock market experts for their opinions. The second group, however, could see only the changes in their stock prices, with no information as to why the prices rose or fell. They had to make trading decisions based on this very limited amount of information.

Would you, like Andreassen, have expected the first group with all that information to earn more than the data-limited second group? Surprisingly, that is not how it turned out. The group with less information earned more than twice as much as the info-rich group. It seems the first group was distracted by too much information. The more data they got, the more difficulty they had separating good advice from bad. They made many trades based on rumors and tips—a guaranteed way to lose money in the stock market.

Imagine conducting a similar study today. With so much financial information available in seconds, one wonders what types of decisions individual investors make. One answer is to look at day traders, those people who make dozens of stock trades a day in the hopes of eking out a little profit on each. David Segal of the *New York Times* cites studies showing that about 80 percent of active individual traders lose money, and only about 1 percent are predictably profitable.[17]

Regretting the Decision

Recall the participants in Dijksterhuis' and Messner's studies: those who made a decision soon after reviewing all the data grew to regret their choice, whereas those with limited information who delayed their decision had no regrets.[18] One of Iyengar's studies supports these results.[19] The study involved students who were doing job searches.

She and her colleagues looked at the amount of information the students collected about an industry (such as prominent companies, the corporate culture, the cities where the companies were located, and average pay and benefits) and their degree of satisfaction with their choices. The researchers discovered that those students who collected a lot of information were less satisfied with their choices than students who collected less information. Apparently, the students who amassed lots of information knew so much about various job possibilities that they could see themselves doing better later in a job that they did not take. And this same regret occurred even when the individual made an objectively better choice. Professor Schwartz at Swarthmore says that when faced with so many choices, decision makers "may do better, but feel worse." To him, "too many choices become paralyzing rather than liberating."[20]

Once again, we have research results that seem counterintuitive. Having collected all that information, shouldn't the students have been pleased with the final choices they made? Schwartz says that depends on a person's goal when making a decision. Based on his research, he suggests that some individuals are *satisficers*, those who look at the options and settle for good enough. Satisficers have standards, and when they find the option that meets those standards, they choose it. They don't fret over their choice or whether there might be something better. They move on. Then there are the *maximizers*, those who want to get the best choice whenever they make a decision. How does one get the best? By searching through all the possibilities—an impossible task even when deciding on jam in a supermarket. At some point, maximizers have to make a decision. Unfortunately, that decision often leads to regret. Regret? How can that be? Surely, with all that information, one should feel secure in the final decision. It doesn't work that way. Maximizers start wondering, "What if I waited a little longer, or collected more data, or studied the options a little harder, might I have made a better choice?" If the choice they made is disappointing, they cannot escape the realization that the poor choice was their fault because, after all, they had plenty of other options available. Over time, the constant feeling of regret and self-blame begins to wear on maximizers—in some cases, to the point of clinical depression. They eventually become regret-aversive and start to avoid making decisions at all.

How to Deal With Information Overload

Before deciding how to handle information overload, you need to be certain that the problem is really too much information as opposed to too much work. Some people misinterpret work overload as information overload. Do your decision makers have too many duties or too many goals to accomplish, or do they waste too much time in excessive travel? If this is the case, then you need to adjust the responsibilities to be more realistic so that you and your colleagues can achieve your goals. If not, then we can look at some strategies that may help you tackle the perils of too much information and too many choices, and ultimately make good decisions. Note that the strategies focus on you taking control of the information environment rather than feeling controlled by it.

Stick to the Relevant

You live in a world in which information systems are constantly throwing more and more facts, figures, and opinions at you. What you really need are systems that filter out unimportant or irrelevant information. The key ingredient in the attention game is relevancy. The brain is always trying to discern patterns and make meaning out of new information. Relevancy makes our attention span stretch a bit further, improving our information-processing capacity and cerebral efficiency so it takes less time and attention resources to acquire the information we really need.

Disregard the Unimportant

Some corporate emails have the same value as junk mail. Devise a method for recognizing them (for example, by name of sender or topic) and send them immediately to the spam folder.

Apportion Your Time Based on Importance

Not every item of information is equally important. Give the most time to those that really matter and skim or ignore the rest.

Prescreen the Information

Consider having all information pass through an assistant who knows your preferences and sends you only the material you need to see. Occasionally look at a sampling of screened-out material to ensure the assistant is following your directions and to avoid becoming isolated.

Divide the Burden

See if there is someone else in the organization who should be getting some of the information instead of you. Divide the overload, and meet with colleagues, when necessary, to share information and work toward a decision.

Practice Chunking

When faced with too much information, the brain attempts to combine items that have similar characteristics—a process known as chunking. Chunking can increase the number of items that working memory can hold. Get that pencil and paper again. Stare at the letters below for seven seconds. Then look away and write them down in the correct sequence and groupings. Ready? Go.

TVI RSCN NF BIU SA

Check your results. Did you get all the letters in the correct sequence and groupings? Probably not. Most people do not score 100 percent on this after looking at the letters for such a short period. Let's try it again with the same rules. Stare for seven seconds and write down the letters below in the same sequence and groupings. Ready? Go.

TV IRS CNN FBI USA

How did you do this time? Probably much better. If you compare the two examples, you will note they are the same letters in the same sequence. What happened here? In the first example, the groupings made little or no sense. Thus, the brain treated each of the fourteen letters and each of the four spaces (because grouping is important) as a separate item, resulting in a total of eighteen items. This total well exceeds working memory's capacity, so you could not remember the example accurately. But in the second example, the brain quickly recognized the five understandable items, and the total was within working memory's capacity. The major difference between the two examples was how the items were chunked. Chunking improves your ability to remember the items. That ability, however, is dependent on your knowledge base. Because the letter combinations were familiar to you, you were able to chunk quickly and accurately. Recall trying to remember that ten-digit number earlier in the chapter. People who spend a lot of time calling others on the telephone often remember all the digits correctly. That's because their brains are accustomed to chunking ten-digit numbers as the area code + prefix + extension, so 9237546302 is quickly represented in the brain as (923) 754-6302. Practice chunking by linking relevant items of information together using some common characteristic, such as their similarities, differences, advantages, disadvantages, functions, or structures.

Accept the Practicality of Satisficing

When there is just too much information and too many choices, resist the search for perfection. Realize that your competitors are in the same overload quagmire as you, and, except in extraordinary circumstances, settle for satisficing. If you do the satisficing in a rational—rather than arbitrary—way, then you have a practical and defensible approach to information management.

Value the Power of Unconscious Thought

You will recall that the studies of Dijksterhuis, Messner, and Iyengar revealed that those participants who got less information, who pondered over it, and who delayed their decisions were much more pleased with their final choices than those who amassed large amounts of data and made a quick decision.[21] For the latter, regret over their choices eventually set in. These results point to the value of unconscious thought. Allowing information to settle and percolate in our unconscious system may ultimately provide the best decision. But too much data can impair the unconscious processes. Loran Nordgren and his colleagues Maarten Bos and Ap Dijksterhuis, for instance, found that when people face a large amount of complex information, they tend to default to their conscious system, a path that often results in poorer choices.[22]

So what's the answer? Do you ignore some of the information and settle for satisficing? In a word, yes. But even that approach can have its challenges; when faced with an information avalanche, your brain has a difficult time deciding which items to ignore. This is especially true when you are gathering information online because every new item links to other new items and so on. Furthermore, it is often difficult to determine the validity and reliability of online information. The researchers suggest that the best strategy, then, may be to use your conscious mind to acquire and screen only the relevant information, move on to some other tasks while the unconscious processes do their work, and then make a decision. With this approach, you are taking advantage of the strengths of both the conscious and unconscious systems and limiting their weaknesses. Several of their studies confirm that the best decisions involving complex choices engage both conscious and unconscious thought and that this sequence is better than conscious or unconscious thought alone. These findings might be difficult to accept because they seem to contradict the notion that the more rational thought given to a complex decision, the better. How do researchers explain this conscious/unconscious paradox?

The Conscious/Unconscious Paradox

As we learn and develop more expertise in our work, the brain builds large and robust information and skill banks in our long-term memory. It also establishes networks that remember the feelings associated with our experiences. Because the emotional brain has a powerful and resilient memory system, we tend to remember the best and worst things that happen to us. We forget mediocre and uneventful experiences quickly. Can you remember what you had for dinner a week ago last Thursday? Probably not, unless it was a special occasion or you got sick from the food. In those instances, the good or bad emotional responses helped you to remember the meal. Whenever you have made an important decision that resulted in a spectacular success or a disappointing failure, your brain retained your feelings of joy or gloom as part of the experience. Over time, these cognitive decisions and their emotional messages form a rich pool of experiences through which you can filter a potential new decision. But that takes time.

The rational brain is very competent at making mundane decisions, such as picking a shirt to wear to work, and at solving simple problems, such as balancing your checkbook. Emotions do not really matter much here. Complex problems are a different story because of their possible consequences. We noted earlier how the prefrontal cortex becomes very inefficient when bombarded by too much information. As a result, you may overanalyze the information and select a choice that you may soon regret (see first example in fig. 1.4, page 22). However, if you use information management strategies to limit the incoming items and avoid rushing to a decision, then your rational brain has the time to explore your pool of experiences and link new information to similar emotion-laden decisions of the past. Now your unconscious thought process can examine options based on your past experiences (assuming you have had a sufficient number of them in your work domain) and render a better decision (see second example in fig. 1.4). This process honors intuition in that the final decision "feels right." Emotional messages play a strong role here, and we will discuss much more about the power of emotions in chapter 3.

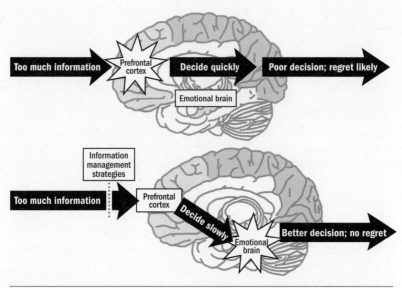

Figure 1.4: In the upper diagram, too much information overloads the prefrontal cortex, resulting in a quick and poor decision followed by regret. In the lower diagram, information management strategies slow down the process and produce a better decision.

A Final Word About Information and the Brain

This chapter has been devoted to deflating the corporate tenet that the more information people have, the better decisions they will make. The reality is that the brain's prefrontal cortex has a limited capacity for information, and when overloaded, it is likely to make a decision that *seems* important but really isn't. In short, *less is more!*

Another pervasive corporate tenet is that modern technology allows employees to multitask, thereby improving their efficiency. Really? Can the brain actually multitask? If so, how does that work? And can employees get better at it? If not, why not? You will find the answers to these questions in the next chapter—and they may surprise you.

CHAPTER TWO

The Myth of Multitasking

There is time enough for everything in the
course of the day, if you do but one thing
at once; but there is not time enough in the
year, if you will do two things at a time.

LORD CHESTERFIELD

IT WAS AROUND NOON, AND THE AIRPORT CLUB LOUNGE WAS PACKED. Bad weather had delayed numerous flights, including mine. People were frantically trying to get in touch with their home offices as well as the clients they were scheduled to meet at their next destination. I could not help but notice the young man sitting across from me; he was talking very loudly into his headset and complaining about the flight delay. But what really caught my attention was how much he was interacting with the items around him. In addition to his headset conversation, he was scrolling through his personal digital assistant and checking his laptop screen, periodically typing a few keystrokes. He also was trying to read a story on the front page of the *USA Today* that was resting on a table next to him. As time went on, he appeared to cycle his attention easily among all the items. Surely, to the casual observer, this man was multitasking. I bet even the man himself believed he was multitasking—but he wasn't. Why? Because the brain cannot multitask.

What Does Multitasking Mean?

Before we go any further, we need to define what the term *multitasking* means in this context. The original definition of multitasking came from the computer industry and referred to a microprocessor's ability to carry out more than one task at a time. Obviously, humans can multitask in that they can simultaneously walk and talk, or ride a bicycle while pondering the beauty of nature, or knit while watching television. We are able to do these tasks concurrently because different parts of the brain are in command of each. Walking, riding a bicycle, and knitting are learned motor skills that are controlled primarily by a structure at the rear base of the brain called the cerebellum (see fig. 2.1). Talking, pondering, and watching television are cognitive operations, which we know are the main responsibility of the prefrontal cortex. As long as we perform tasks that call on two brain regions with separate responsibilities, we are able to carry them out successfully. But when we call on the same part of the brain to carry out two or more functions simultaneously, problems arise.

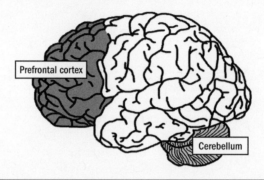

Figure 2.1: The prefrontal cortex deals with cognitive processing. The cerebellum controls motor movements, balance, and equilibrium.

Let's demonstrate this notion with a simple but amusing motor skills activity. Sit in a chair, lift your right leg, and move it in clockwise circles for several seconds. Stop. Place your right foot back on the floor. Now extend your right arm and your right index finger. Use this finger to draw the number 8 continuously for several seconds. Stop. Now lift your right leg and move it in clockwise circles while at the same time drawing the number 8 with your right hand. How did you do? Did you lose control of either your leg or your hand movements?

What happened here? You were able to perform each of the movements separately. However, as soon as you tried to do them together, you were calling on the cerebellum to control two unrelated motor tasks simultaneously—a feat it cannot do. The neural signals got scrambled, and you lost control. Similar results will occur when the prefrontal cortex encounters the same predicament. Ever try to talk on the phone and write an email at the same time? Those cognitive activities are almost impossible to do together. For the purposes of this discussion, multitasking refers to calling on the same brain region to carry out more than one task simultaneously.

Survival Requires Focus

Remember, the brain's main task is to keep its owner alive. Survival requires the ability to focus intently on incoming signals that could pose a threat to the individual. Those ancestors of ours who were unable to do so most likely ended up as some predator's lunch; their genes never entered the gene pool. On the other hand, the individuals who were able to concentrate on a threat and find ways to avoid or defeat it were more apt to live long enough to find a mate and transmit that focusing ability to their offspring—and a few hundred millennia later, to us.

Torkel Klingberg, a cognitive neuroscientist at the Karolinska Institute in Sweden, has conducted experiments with brain scans that indicate that a certain region of the brain (known as the *globus pallidus*) is highly active when individuals are fending off distractions.[1] Think of this area as a nightclub bouncer, preventing irrelevant items from getting into the club called working memory. This makes sense. Focus equals survival. When a car is speeding toward you in the wrong lane and a head-on collision is imminent, you do not want your brain's attention systems shifting suddenly to admiring the colorful flowers on the roadside trees or wondering whether the car needs a new set of tires.

In 2009, when Captain Chesley Sullenberger was piloting his disabled jet over the Hudson River with 155 passengers and crew on board, he knew that focus was his only hope. He didn't even pray. "I imagine somebody in back was taking care of that for me," he told Katie Couric of CBS News. "My focus was so intensely on landing, I thought of nothing else." In the three minutes he had from the time the plane started its unrelenting descent until it hit water, Sullenberger screened out all external input and relied on his forty years of flying experience to guide the sixty-ton aircraft. After a bumpy landing on the water's surface, he said to his copilot, "Well, that wasn't as bad as I thought."[2] Thanks to his focusing ability, not one life was lost.

Safety experts advise against using a cell phone while driving because they want drivers to avoid distractions during cognitive activities. Talking on a cell phone requires significant cognitive resources. About 70 percent of a face-to-face conversation involves nonverbal communication, such as facial expressions, body gestures, posture, and degree of eye contact, all of which carry meaning. In the absence of these nonverbal cues—such as during a phone call—the brain has to work harder by analyzing the caller's voice for tone, pitch, and pacing to determine the true meaning and intent of the caller's words. This is not easy because even the best technology does not faithfully transmit all the characteristics of a person's voice. Such diversion of attention resources—about 37 percent, according to the fMRI scans—significantly reduces the driver's response time and ability to make quick decisions when the car in front suddenly brakes or another car unexpectedly changes lanes. Research studies conducted by David Strayer and his colleagues at the University of Utah and neuroscientist Marcel Just at Carnegie Mellon University have shown that the cognitive impairments that occur when using a cell phone while driving are as serious as those associated with driving while drunk.[3] That's scary. If you are thinking that hands-free or voice-activated cell phones are safer, you are mistaken. These studies showed that they made little difference in the driver's level of distraction.

Does talking to someone in the car involve the same amount of distraction? No. Strayer's research found that although talking with a passenger involves some diversion of attention, it is far less than the distraction of a phone conversation. In the car, you can hear all the characteristics of the passenger's voice, and your eyes may catch direct or peripheral views of the speaker, helping you assess those important nonverbal signals. In short, it is a lot easier for your brain to determine the meaning and intent of the passenger's words in the car than those of the caller on the phone. Furthermore, the passenger is an extra set of eyes to alert you to road hazards.

What about texting and driving? Well, let's see. I am going to be driving a vehicle, a task that requires the full attention of my eyes and extensive coordination of my hands. Oh, and at the same time, I am going to be texting a message, a task that requires considerable attention from my eyes and intricate coordination of my fingers. Is there a problem with that? This combination is not only dangerous, it is insane!

The Costs of Tasking

If the man in the airport lounge is not multitasking, then what is he doing? When the brain has to attend to multiple items in working memory, one option is to shift its focus back and forth between two items at astonishing speeds. This is called *alternate tasking*. Or, the brain can shift its focus among more than two items, a process called *sequential tasking*. Figure 2.2 illustrates the two options.

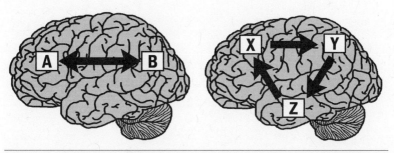

Figure 2.2: The left diagram shows alternate tasking as the brain shifts its attention from A to B and back to A. The right diagram shows sequential tasking, with attention shifting from X to Y to Z and back to X.

The brain of our airport executive is probably using both methods. He is doing alternate tasking when, for example, his attention moves from the newspaper to the digital assistant and then to the paper again. If he were to get a phone call about a change in a meeting date, he would likely engage in sequential tasking. He would focus first on the caller's message (X in fig. 2.2), turn to the digital assistant to send a text message to his office advising of the new date (Y), and then focus on his laptop to alter the dates in his slide presentation (Z). Then he could tell the caller that he made the necessary changes (back to X).

At this point, you might be thinking, "So what? Does it make any difference that multitasking is really alternate or sequential tasking? Isn't the result the same—namely, that I can accomplish two tasks at about the same time?" Sorry, you may wish that to be true, but it is not.

Try this simple activity that demonstrates how alternate tasking causes cognitive problems. Get ready to count as quickly as you can from one to ten. Ready? Go! That probably took you about two seconds. Now get ready to recite the alphabet letters from A to J quickly. Ready? Go! That also took you around two seconds. If we put these two tasks together, one after the other, it would take you four seconds to complete. Instead, I would like you to interweave the two tasks as fast as you can, that is, A, 1, B, 2, and so on. Ready? Go! Now that likely took you fifteen to twenty seconds, and you may have made some errors. Your brain had to continually shift from the alphabet task to the counting task and back again. This constant shifting between or among items in working memory comes at a cognitive cost not only in time, but also in accuracy and attention. Figure 2.3 (page 28) helps explain why this is so.

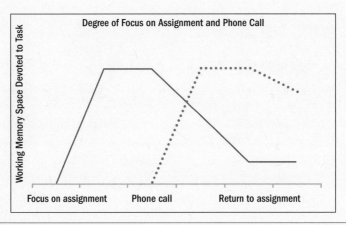

Figure 2.3: The solid line shows an increase in working memory processing for the assignment. As soon as attention shifts to the phone call, indicated by the dotted line, memory resources devoted to the assignment drop as memory resources are used to begin processing information from the caller.

Say you are in your office, working intently on your computer to complete an important assignment for the CEO. The rise in the solid line in figure 2.3 shows how your working memory is devoting its full resources to processing the assignment. Recall that working memory has a limited capacity. Your cell phone rings. The caller ID indicates that your spouse is at the other end. You think, "Hmmm, I'd better answer it." As soon as you do, attention resources shift from your assignment to the phone call. Signals from the emotional brain facilitate this shift because, after all, the caller is your spouse, and there may be emotional consequences later for not answering the call. Notice in figure 2.3 how the solid line (resources associated with your assignment) drops rapidly, while the dotted line—representing the resources dedicated to the phone call—rises quickly. When the call ends, working memory has pushed out much of what you were working on for the assignment to make room for the items discussed in your spouse's call. Returning to your assignment, you realize that you do not remember much of what you were working on at the time of the call, and you think, "OK, where was I?"

This dramatic loss of attention occurs every time you switch your focus to another source of information, such as answering a phone call or an email. Researchers call this the *task switch cost*, and these costs add up. Often, working memory gets fatigued from this constant shifting and pays less attention to new information—another reason why too much information paralyzes working memory. Brain scans confirm how easily nonrelevant stimuli, such as the spouse's phone call, can disrupt our concentration. Using fMRI, researcher Katherine Moore and her colleagues at the University of Michigan found that irrelevant cues introduced when a person was concentrating on relevant information literally hijacked the attention systems, causing resources to be diverted to processing the unrelated items.[4] Amazingly, these constant interruptions can have a lasting effect on our brainpower.

Attempts at Multitasking Can Dumb You Down

Research studies at the Institute of Psychiatry of King's College London, led by Glenn Wilson, looked at the mental concentration levels of 1,100 office workers.[5] They found that excessive use of technology actually reduced workers' intelligence. Individuals who were distracted by incoming phone calls or emails had an astounding ten-point drop in their IQ—more than twice that found in studies of the impact of marijuana use on intelligence. Participants who had a lack of discipline in handling emails had the largest IQ loss. Many workers had an almost addictive compulsion to reply to each new message, resulting in constant changes in focus and the eventual fatigue of the prefrontal cortex. Their attempts at being more productive were, in reality, seriously undermining their productivity. Curiously, 90 percent of the participants agreed that it was rude to receive and handle messages during office meetings or face-to-face conversations. Nonetheless, about a third of them said that this had become an acceptable practice because they believed their supervisors interpreted their behavior as a sign of diligence and efficiency.

Attempts at Multitasking Adversely Affect Long-Term Memory

There is growing research evidence that consistent attempts at multitasking affect our brain's ability to encode information into long-term memory. Psychologist Karin Foerde and her colleagues at the University of California, Los Angeles used fMRI scans to observe the brains of participants as they were learning and trying to remember numerous tasks.[6] One group learned their tasks without distractions, whereas the other group had their learning interrupted with distracting beeps—not unlike those we hear from cell phones or arriving emails. Later, the researchers asked both groups to recall what they had learned. The undistracted group was able to recall significantly more of what they learned than the distracted group, an indication that distractions interfere with learning and memory. Looking at brain scans while both groups were engaged in learning revealed that the part of the brain responsible for encoding long-term memories (the hippocampus) was active in the undistracted group but inactive in the distracted group. The researchers concluded that attempts at multitasking change the way we learn and diminish what we remember.

Attempts at Multitasking Hinder Working Memory in Older People

One of the more disturbing research findings on how multitasking might affect the brain comes from a study comparing how the working memories of older and younger individuals respond to interruptions in their work. Wesley Clapp, Adam Gazzaley, and their colleagues, neurologists at the University of California, San Francisco, found that attempts at multitasking took a significantly greater toll on the working memory of the older participants (ages sixty to eighty) than the younger ones (in their twenties and thirties).[7] Their study examined how long it took the participants to remember and refocus on a task after a brief interruption. Older participants found it much more difficult to disengage from the interruption and reestablish contact with their original task. This may partially explain why older folks can walk to the refrigerator and then stand at the door trying to remember what they were going to get or go to the supermarket for bread and come back with twenty other items but not bread.

Intrigued with this finding, the researchers added fMRI scans to determine what brain regions were at work. The brains of younger and older people showed distinct differences in activity following an interruption. In the younger participants, the brain areas disengaged from the interruption more quickly than did those of the older participants. Apparently, the older group had a diminished ability to reactivate the brain networks involved in the original task. The study is significant because aging adults are spending more time in workplaces that have high technological demands and frequent interruptions. Could these results indicate that as younger people spend more time in a multitasking world, their working memory capacity may diminish more as they age than it would were they not in that environment? And if interruptions make it difficult to retain items in working memory, especially for older people, could this diminish their ability to retain those experiences in long-term memory? Further research may answer these questions.

Can I Train Myself to Multitask?

Based on what you have already learned about the effects of attempting to multitask, why would you even want to try? OK, this is a trick question. We already know that the brain cannot multitask, at least not as we have defined it here—the ability of the same brain region to perform multiple tasks simultaneously. Just because you have been doing what *seems* like multitasking for a long time, that does not mean you are good at it. However, this notion does seem to run counter to Malcolm Gladwell's claim that the key to success is largely due to practicing a particular task for about 10,000 hours.[8] Is it possible that individuals who identify themselves as high-multitaskers have been practicing for so long that they have acquired certain skills that have altered their brains so that they can *actually* process two cognitive things at once? Researchers at Stanford University, led by Eyal Ophir, decided to test this possibility.[9] The researchers speculated that high-multitaskers might have substantially developed one or more of the abilities to:

- Filter out irrelevant information
- Switch rapidly from one task to the other
- Keep information neatly organized in working memory

After repeated experiments with more than 260 participants, it turned out that the supposed high-multitaskers were terrible at all three. Follow-up experiments showed that multitaskers were also worse at analytical reasoning.[10] These results are particularly worrisome because children are getting involved in multitasking at younger ages and may be developing habits that can cause cognitive problems later. Preadolescents who are not able to screen out irrelevant material, or go from one task to another, or organize their memory systems are going to face difficulties in school, college, and the workplace.

If multitaskers are really not good at it, why don't they stop? Mainly because they believe they *are* good at it! That is what the multitaskers told the researchers at Stanford. Furthermore, they were completely unfazed by multitasking and convinced that they could do even more. Some multitaskers, especially students and businesspeople, say that they must do six things at once because it would take too long to do them one at a time. The research studies do not support this contention. These people would accomplish much more if they completed one task, then completed the next, and so on. Instead, by multitasking, they are not thinking clearly, and they are not completing any item well. In other words, those who do too many things at one time are *less competent* at what they are doing than those who do fewer things at once. This is a case where practice does not make perfect. In fact, the more you practice multitasking, the worse you are at it.

Aren't I Using Only 10 Percent of My Brain?

When I mentioned the myth of multitasking to one executive recently, his response was, "I thought we use only 10 percent of our brain. Isn't some of that other 90 percent available to do more tasks at once?" Unfortunately, that executive had fallen for another myth about the brain that simply refuses to die. No one seems to know exactly where this idea started. Some historians attribute it to a misinterpretation of the work of the late-nineteenth-century psychologist William James, who often wrote about how many people achieve only a small portion of their potential. Others may have later morphed his idea into "10 percent of our capacity" and ultimately to "10 percent of our brain."

Regardless of the myth's origin, it is false, news that may come as a disappointment to those who would like to think that there is the potential for significantly increasing our brainpower by waking up that supposedly dormant 90 percent. Brain scans have clearly shown that all parts of a living brain are active all of the time. Some areas are usually *more* active than others when the individual is performing a certain task. For example, there are brain regions on the left side of the brain that specialize in processing language. Those areas would show up as more active than others in an fMRI scan when the subject is speaking or reading. The good news is that neuroscientists are discovering some ways in which we can boost our brainpower, thanks to *neuroplasticity*—the brain's ability to change some functions and structures in response to input. We will discuss these fascinating findings in chapter 7.

Is There Any Hope of Training Your Brain to Really Multitask?

The answer to this question is maybe yes, maybe no. Some psychologists suggest that because the young brain is so flexible, it may be possible to train youngsters to truly multitask at an early age. That ability, however, is still limited by how fast the prefrontal cortex can process information.

An interesting research question is whether you can train your brain to increase its processing speed so it would be possible to perform two tasks at once. To answer this question, Paul Dux and a research team at Vanderbilt University ran an experiment to determine whether they could speed up cognitive processing.[11] They found that, with training, the brain could perform cognitive tasks faster, thus allowing time for another task. At first, the participants multitasked poorly, but later they were able to perform the tasks seemingly simultaneously. Brain scans, however, indicated that although the prefrontal cortex was processing information faster, the brain was not truly multitasking. Events were happening faster but not at once. Researchers will, no doubt, continue to pursue this line of inquiry. In the meantime, let's focus on stemming the flow of information, much of it irrelevant to your tasks.

Ignoring Irrelevant Information

The brain's ability to focus under the right circumstances is very impressive. Despite the ability of irrelevant information to co-opt some of the brain's attentional resources, we can train the prefrontal cortex to ignore these distractions, especially recurring ones—but it takes effort. For example, a commuter traveling to and from work every day on a train eventually learns to focus on reading her newspaper and to screen out the clickety-clack noise of the train and the conversations of those around her. She trains her brain to give priority to visual information and to ignore auditory information. This capability can be very useful in various circumstances. I once rented an apartment close to railroad tracks. Trains would pass by at all hours, often waking me in the

Are There Gender Differences in Multitasking?

Researchers have known for a long time that females are better at *physical* multitasking than men. This is a result of the evolutionary roles of males and females. Our male ancestors' main task was to hunt for food—a difficult and dangerous task on the savanna. As the men were looking for animals as food, many of the animals saw the men as food. Apart from hunting, there were the occasional male-to-male skirmishes to protect their food stashes, caves, or mates. The demands on their brains for coordinating physical tasks were limited and focused. Females, on the other hand, usually had to cook the food, clean the cave, rear the children, and devise games to keep the children near the cave and out of the way of hungry predators. These demands helped them develop the capability for physical multitasking much better than men. Neither males nor females, however, evolved a brain to deal with the onslaught of today's information world. Consequently, researchers find no difference between males and females when it comes to cognitive multitasking. Both genders are equally bad at it.

middle of the night. After several weeks, my brain learned to screen out those train noises, and I slept peacefully from then on.

This ability to focus intently on relevant items while ignoring irrelevant ones does not prevent you from responding to unusual, important, and intense background stimuli. When the train commuter hears the name of her station stop on the loudspeaker, she prepares to get off. Whenever trains screeched to a halt outside my apartment window, I awoke quickly and speculated about what caused the unexpected stop. Certain stimuli always get our attention. Your child might be on a playground with dozens of other children all yelling in delight. But if your child gets injured and cries in pain, that sound will get past all others in your brain and grab your attention.

Today, the ring of a cell phone has the same priority as the screeching of the train brakes or your child's cries. Our culture has trained us to respond to a ringing phone. That is why you would not be able to resist interrupting your concentration on a work assignment to look at your cell phone's caller ID. The best way to ignore irrelevant information is to keep it out of your immediate work environment. The message here is simple: focus on one thing, and switch the irrelevant technology off.

Peter Bregman, an adviser to CEOs, tells the story of what happened to him when he decided to abandon all multitasking for a week.[12] He interacted with only one technology at a time. If he was on the phone or at a meeting, his entire focus was on the caller or the presenter. He held off any interruptions until he finished what he was working on. Six revelations came out of this weeklong experiment. As you look at these, consider whether any of them would make your work more productive and your life more enjoyable.

1. **More time with significant others**. Technology disengages you from your family and friends. It used to be that one of the best gifts you could give someone was your complete attention. Doing so signaled that you respected what the person had to say or do and that this human and personal interaction was important. Not responding to every ring of the cell phone or every ding of an incoming email gives you the time you need to devote your full attention to those you care about. You engage more deeply in conversations with them and learn more about their cares and hopes.

2. **More time to follow through on challenging projects**. Tough projects require deep thinking and persistence—not easy to do with constant interruptions. Focusing on a challenging task without distraction can often lead to the breakthrough you need to take it to successful completion.

3. **Lower stress levels**. Trying to do too many things at once raises anxiety in your brain, causing the adrenal gland to release *cortisol*, a steroid designed to focus the brain on determining the source of the stress and deciding how to respond. To accomplish this, the prefrontal cortex shuts down the processing of any items not directly related to diminishing or eliminating the source of the stress. The presence of cortisol also accounts for the fatigue and irritability you experience when you try to keep too many balls in the air at once. However, the feeling of accomplishment you experience when you finish one project before going on to the next greatly reduces stress.

4. **Low tolerance for wasted time**. When there are no interruptions, you become laser-focused on carrying out your work. Wandering conversations and overly long meetings are wearisome. You want to get back to work and solve problems.

5. **High tolerance for useful and enjoyable experiences**. Relaxing conversations with your spouse and children become much more enjoyable. When there are no interruptions from technology, you can really focus on doing personal things that you enjoy.

6. **No downside**. You lose nothing by avoiding attempts at multitasking and resisting interruptions. You will actually complete projects with greater efficiency and less frustration. Moreover, you will probably discover that no one will get angry that you did not answer a phone call or instantly reply to an email; others will be too busy dealing with their own tasks. Besides, very few of the messages are truly urgent.

Consider barring technology at meetings. If it is your meeting, you should be the one getting the attention. You can use whatever technology you need to make your presentation, but everyone else should come empty-handed. That way, the focus is exclusively on you. No interruptions, no secretive texting under the table, no Facebook dalliances on the laptops—only you. If you should not be the focus of attention, then why have the meeting in the first place? There can be a few exceptions, but very few. You will be doing your colleagues a genuine favor—giving them freedom from technological interruptions for the length of the meeting. They may even thank you.

Are you willing to try this? Can you find the courage to eliminate interruptions for a week and focus on doing just one important cognitive task at a time? If so, you may experience the same rewards Bregman noted, and that may encourage you to continue this new approach for a longer period. Eliminating interruptions will not be easy to accomplish. Work environments and cultural forces are continually increasing the trend toward more multitasking. Some workplaces are now requiring their employees to answer emails within fifteen minutes of receipt. You may be distracted by the 100,000-plus software applications for smartphones and smart pads, or the 100 million videos on YouTube. And, what about tweets and messages from Facebook and other social media sites? Do they frequently entice you as well? Avoiding the temptation to multitask is a difficult challenge in today's fast-paced, information-overloaded culture. The irony is that all this seemingly progressive technology may be thrusting us into a world that the human brain is totally unprepared to handle.

A Final Word About Multitasking

Perhaps our brains can save us after all. Remember, whenever the rational brain gets overloaded, the emotional brain often steps in to lend assistance. As we saw in chapter 1, input from the emotional brain helps us reach a better and more satisfying decision than we would reach without it. Yet pundits have told us to keep emotions out of business decisions. That may be the worst advice ever. Our journey through the next chapter explains why.

CHAPTER THREE

Respecting the Emotional Brain

Emotions have taught mankind to reason.

MARQUIS DE VAUVENARGUES

SHALL I STAY, OR SHALL I QUIT? THAT WAS ONE OF THE MOST DIFFICULT questions I have had to consider in my career. Do I follow my head and stay in this CEO position, or do I follow my gut and get out? Have you ever been in that situation? If so, you know about those sleepless nights when the pros and cons of such a life-changing move are racing through your brain. The cerebral conflict can be disquieting and exhausting. It is especially daunting when logic screams out to stay and there is no other job waiting for you. Quitting means the end of a salary, along with the important benefits and perquisites that go with it. I had to decide between my rational brain's need for security and my emotional brain's urge to say, "Screw it! Leave!"

I was the superintendent of a small, upper-middle-class school district in the northeast. Everything went well the first two years. Parents were pleased with new courses that were academically more challenging. Teachers were energized over the revised professional development program that focused on long-term, job-embedded training rather than on irrelevant one-hour sessions. Students were happy with new state-of-the-art computers in the schools. The central office support staff were eager to transfer reports, records, and data from paper to computers. To accommodate the increasing student population, the community approved a bond issue to expand all of the schools. Things were really humming.

In the beginning, the board of education supported my initiatives, because all of the members had hired me. They stuck to their main role as policymakers and left it to me to run the district. But after two school board elections, five of the seven original members had been replaced. Several of the newly elected members had a different view of their role, deciding that micromanaging the district and politicking were much more fun than just making policy. Board meetings were becoming contentious and less productive.

In my third year (I had a five-year contract), I was spending most of my time fending off ill-advised and inappropriate proposals from board members, and my effectiveness was waning. I was in a quandary. I looked at the logic of staying: a decent salary, excellent benefits, strong parental and teacher support, good rapport with my colleagues and subordinates, and significant progress toward expanding the district's buildings. These were all very strong logical reasons to stay and tough it out. My rational brain was pleased as punch! But my emotional brain was in turmoil. Advice from significant others sided mostly with logic. I spent a ten-day winter recess on a Florida beach mentally refereeing the battle between my rational and emotional brains. Despite that think time in the sun, I returned home undecided.

The Rational and Emotional Brains

Our rational and emotional brains process information differently and, thus, give us alternative perspectives of the same situation. In children, the emotional brain (the limbic system) has much more influence over the rational brain (the prefrontal cortex) than in adults. Figure 3.1 helps explain why. The emotional brain develops faster than the rational brain, but one of the main responsibilities of the prefrontal cortex is to keep emotional responses under control. This developmental lag between the two brains is significant. In most individuals, the emotional brain matures between the ages of ten and twelve, whereas the rational brain matures between the ages of twenty-two and twenty-four. This ten- to twelve-year lag in the development of the rational brain explains why adolescents and young adults often make decisions based on emotions and why they are prone to risky behavior. In mature adults, the rational brain keeps the emotional brain in check most of the time. As we gain more experience, our emotions detect patterns and construct appropriate responses to common situations. Cultural norms, along with society's expectations and laws, dictate many of these responses: keep your cool when waiting your turn in line or when getting cut off on the highway by an erratic driver; remember to say "thank you" to the store clerk, whether you mean it or not; and so on.

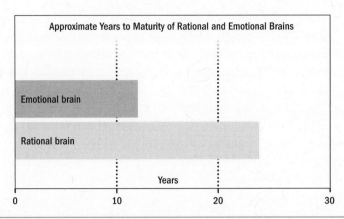

Figure 3.1: The emotional brain matures at around the age of eleven, and the rational brain (prefrontal cortex) matures at around the age of twenty-three.

Before the 1990s, psychologists believed that all brain signals from outside stimuli went first to the prefrontal cortex and then to the limbic area, which then sent signals out to the rest of the body to determine the appropriate response. In the early 1990s, neuroscientist Joseph LeDoux, then at the Cornell University Medical Center in New York City, made a startling discovery.[1] Experimenting with animals, he found a small bundle of neurons that sent some incoming signals directly to a limbic structure called the *amygdala* (Greek for *almond*, because of its size and shape). The amygdala is mainly involved in the processing of emotions, determining emotional responses, and encoding emotional memories. This shorter backdoor pathway is separate from the major pathway to the prefrontal cortex. It allows the amygdala to receive input directly from the senses and generate a response even before the prefrontal cortex has fully interpreted the signals. This means that the emotional brain can trigger a response before the rational brain has vetted it for appropriateness.

Say, for example, you are walking in the woods, and you see a large snake on the path ahead of you. Visual signals travel to the sensory processing and switching center called the *thalamus*. Most are then sent to the brain's visual processing region at the back of the brain for interpretation and response. If the response is emotional, a signal goes to the amygdala to activate the emotional areas. Meanwhile, a portion of the original signal is sent via the backdoor pathway directly from the thalamus to the amygdala, allowing for a quicker, though less precise, response. You are already vacating the area near the snake before the rational brain fully realizes what is happening. The emotional system has taken control of your responses before you are consciously aware of it. Fortunately, in this instance, the hijacking of the rational brain had a good outcome; your rapid response may have prevented a bite from a poisonous snake.

But it does not always work out that way. In highly charged and unusually frightening situations, the body floods the brain with arousing chemicals, such as cortisol and dopamine, overwhelming the prefrontal cortex. Signals zap across the limbic neurons at incredible speeds, often in total confusion. If the emotional brain is fully primed but the rational brain has no clue how to respond, the situation can result in tragedy.

Saturday, October 25, 2003, was a typical warm night in suburban south Florida. Mark Drewes, a tall high school sophomore, had just celebrated his sixteenth birthday. Across the street was the home of Jay Levin, a slight forty-year-old man who lived alone and worked as an accountant. It was after midnight, and Drewes was in an impish mood. He and a friend decided to play an early Halloween prank by ringing their neighbors' doorbells and running away. Drewes went to Levin's porch and stood outside the front door. Hearing noises at that late hour, Levin was frightened. He told police later that he was sure someone was trying to break in and that he was fearful for his life. Instead of calling 911, Levin grabbed his .40-caliber handgun, opened the door, and saw a large shadowy figure. Convinced the figure was reaching for a gun, Levin fired one shot, fatally injuring the boy. Emotions had so clouded his judgment that when he recounted the incident for the police at the scene, he left out one critically important fact: Drewes was shot in the back. The boy was unarmed and running away, posing no threat. Yet Levin pulled the trigger. How could this happen? Neighbors in this low-crime neighborhood described Levin as a quiet man, and police records showed that he had never been in trouble with the law. Why didn't he just call 911 and let the police handle it? Apparently, Levin's rational mind never had time to consider that option. Emotional signals escalated and overwhelmed his reason. Concern led to fear, fear led to panic, and panic led to tragedy.[2]

Keeping emotions under control in these kinds of circumstances is very difficult but not impossible. Captain Sullenberger had only three minutes to set his disabled plane down on the Hudson River.[3] In contrast to Levin, he did not have time to let his fear turn to panic. Instead, thanks to his training and experience, he was able to tune out his feelings. Pilots call this the "deliberate calm." His prefrontal cortex took control, and the only words out of his mouth during those terrifying moments were: "Brace for impact." Similarly, Bill Driscoll, a former fighter pilot and Top Gun instructor, has described how he maintained that laser-sharp focus despite the stress and danger of flying a jet at 700 miles per hour at 100 feet of altitude, while being pursued by enemy planes.[4] Both Sullenberger and Driscoll have their training to thank for continuing to think logically and act deliberately even as their emotional system was attempting to hijack their reasoning abilities.

Emotional Messages Get Attention

Most of the time, our rational and emotional brains work together. They send messages back and forth, assessing and interpreting incoming stimuli for threats, patterns, and meaning, and deciding what response, if any, to make. Recall that the brain gives its immediate attention to incoming information that signals a potential threat to survival. No matter how enthralled you are with this book, if you hear an emergency vehicle's siren outside your window, your attention will shift to that sound even though your eyes may be still moving across the page. In those few moments, the rational and emotional brains are communicating and listening to the pitch and volume of the siren. As soon as the siren sound passes, your brain signals an "all clear," and your attention returns to the printed page. If, on the other hand, the siren sound gets louder and suddenly stops, the brain signals a "better check this out," and you will likely go to the window and investigate.

Emotions come in many varieties, from anger, fear, and sadness to happiness and love. Different emotions prepare the body for different responses. Fear, for example, causes a release of cortisol and adrenaline, hormones that divert blood to our muscles, making it easier to flee and getting our body ready to react. When we are angry, blood diverts to the hands, in case we need to throw a punch or grab a weapon. Sadness causes a drop in our metabolism and promotes internal reflection on our loss and grief.

Recall that, after survival input, emotional messages get next priority. As much as we would like to believe that we are essentially rational beings, we are truly emotional beings first. How we *feel* about a situation nearly always precedes what we *think* about it. In fact, when we ask most people what they *think* about something, their first response usually includes more emotion-laden words ("I like/dislike/feel . . .") than rational-based words ("It is reasonable/logical/sensible . . .").

We do not realize how much the emotional brain influences our behavior. For example, when you are walking toward someone you are meeting for the first time and know little about, your emotional brain is rapidly sizing up that person. Is his facial expression threatening, neutral, or submissive? (Interpreting facial expressions was so vital to our ancestors' survival that we have an area of our brain dedicated to this task.) Are his eyes looking directly at your eyes or averted? Is his stride hesitant or confident? Is he leaning forward or walking upright? Are his clothes appropriate for the occasion? In those few seconds, you have formed an unconscious impression of how you feel about this person. This happens in milliseconds, and you are not even aware of it.

Sometimes referred to as the *cognitive subconscious*, our emotions have a mind of their own, and their opinion may be quite different from that of the rational mind. During your conversation with this new acquaintance, your emotional and rational brains collect and exchange more information about him that will confirm ("See, I knew he was a jerk") or modify ("Actually, he's quite bright") or, on a few occasions, contradict ("I was totally wrong about him!") your initial unconscious impression. These assessments are rooted in our evolutionary past and are the emotional brain's way of determining whether a stranger poses a threat. With practice and a variety of experiences with people, your emotional brain gets better at assessing the intentions of others. Can this same scrutiny by your emotional brain also help you in the decision-making process? The answer is yes.

The Emotional Brain and the Decision-Making Process

Let's say you make an important prediction or decision that turns out to be an error. Recognition of the mistake activates your brain's *anterior cingulate cortex* (ACC), a region that is involved in the detection of errors. The ACC generates a special electrical signal called *error-related negativity* (see fig. 3.2). Because your error was an unexpected outcome, the ACC focuses on it and sends signals to other parts of the brain, such as the thalamus, which directs your conscious attention to the error. Other ACC signals activate the hypothalamus, which sends adrenaline into your bloodstream, increasing your heart rate and tightening your muscles. Consequently, your disappointment over the error becomes a strong emotional event, and you will likely get angry with yourself. Neuroscientists refer to this sequence as the "Oh, shit!" circuit. The ACC monitors the interaction between what you

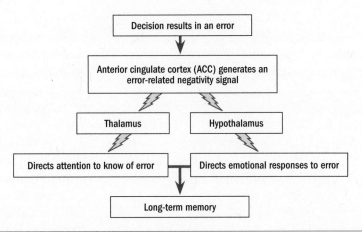

Figure 3.2: This diagram illustrates how the brain responds to a decision-making error. Both the knowledge of the error and how you feel about it are remembered so that you learn from your mistakes.

know of the error and how you *feel* about it. Finally, signals activate the hippocampus and the amygdala to encode this experience into long-term memory. The former encodes the cognitive information, such as the facts and figures of the decision, and the latter encodes the emotions associated with it. From this point forward, the lesson you learned from this experience will be useful input when making future decisions. If this cognitive-emotional memory storage did not take place, we would never learn from our mistakes and, thus, be destined to repeat them.

James Dyson, the inventor of the bag-less vacuum cleaner, tells of making about 5,000 design mistakes over a five-year period. What little he learned from each mistake made the next iteration a bit better, until he was able to settle on a machine that worked to his specifications. Although his cleaners are successful worldwide, he is still modifying and improving them. As Dyson puts it, "I love mistakes."[5]

Emotional Intelligence

At first look, the term *emotional intelligence* may seem like an oxymoron along the lines of *jumbo shrimp* or *virtual reality*. On the contrary, it is a very serious area of study, and it has nothing to do with warm fuzzies or some of the dubious self-help infomercials that air on late-night television. For many years, conventional wisdom was to avoid emotions when making important decisions. In our society, the term *emotional* is often associated with being weak or behaving childishly.

Recently, however, researchers have suggested that the brain's ability to link emotions with the cognitive systems of the prefrontal cortex involved in decision making may actually produce better decisions.

Recall from chapter 1 how Dijksterhuis' buyers who delayed their decision were much more pleased with their purchase than those who made a quick decision.[6] That time delay gave the emotional brain the opportunity to add its input to the cognitive mix, resulting in a better and more satisfying choice. However, emotional intelligence, or EI, varies in individuals. Specifically, EI describes one's ability to perceive and understand emotions, use emotions to facilitate thought processes, and manage emotions to enhance personal success. Psychologist Daniel Goleman's 1995 seminal book on this topic explained how people who can thoroughly understand their emotions and manage them appropriately for each situation are 85 percent more likely to be successful in their job and life decisions than those who are poor at it.[7] In other words, those with high EI have a considerable advantage over those with a lower EI.

Habits of People With High EI

A search through the research literature turned up the following habits exhibited by people who score high in tests of EI. The list is not definitive, but it provides a good overview. People with high EI do the following:

- Validate the feelings of others
- Show respect for the feelings of others
- Use their emotions to help make important decisions
- Take responsibility for their feelings
- Clearly distinguish between cognitive information and feelings
- Avoid controlling, blaming, or judging others
- Look for a positive outcome from their negative emotions

Researchers in this area claim that high-EI individuals are less stressed, more successful in the workplace, and happier, and lead more contented lives. Curiously, studies seem to show little correlation between EI and IQ. People can be intellectually smart but have low EI, and vice versa. A person with low EI may be in an important position, but he or she is seldom a leader.

I worked for a while in the US Foreign Service—America's diplomatic corps. My first assignment was to our mission to the United Nations European headquarters in Geneva, specifically to the International

Disarmament Conference. At that time, we were working with the Soviet Union on a treaty to ban nuclear weapons from the seabed. The Soviet Union had begun exploring a technology that would allow weapons to be placed in the seabed, which would constitute a potential threat to our nuclear deterrence efforts. Because the treaty involved complicated scientific and technical discussions, diplomats and scientists were flying into Geneva on a regular basis.

One regular visitor was a fellow diplomat—let's call him Roland—who impressed me because he was a quiet man who lacked the inflated ego of some of our colleagues. He was an expert in Soviet relations, had a PhD in Russian history, and spoke fluent Russian as well as several other languages. By all accounts, he was brilliant, and he often gave our delegates tips about Soviet culture that proved advantageous during the face-to-face negotiations. Yet, in the two years we were in Geneva, he was never once part of the US team that sat down with the Soviet team to negotiate the treaty. Although this continually puzzled me, I assumed it had to do with higher-ranking diplomats wanting the glory and the promotions that followed the signing of such an important treaty. The negotiations were long and difficult, mainly because the Soviets could not agree on methods for verifying compliance. Fortunately, an international treaty was signed a year later, and our lead negotiator told me that Roland had mapped out cognitive strategies and suggested cleverly worded treaty language in Russian regarding verification that helped break the deadlock. When I asked why Russian-speaking Roland never participated in the negotiating sessions, all I got for an answer was a shrug of the shoulders.

Sometime later, I unexpectedly met Roland at a diplomatic reception in Washington, DC. He was sitting alone at a table in the corner of the large hotel ballroom. As I walked over to greet him, I noticed he was pale and sweating profusely. After saying hello, I asked if he was ill. He assured me he was fine, just very uncomfortable with the setting. When I suggested we mingle with the crowd (as diplomats are expected to do), he reluctantly agreed. After watching him interact with others, I suddenly realized why he was never part of the negotiating sessions in Geneva. Roland had no people skills. He had difficulty starting or maintaining a conversation, had an expressionless face, showed no emotion, and did not respond to the emotions of others.

You would think social skills would be an important prerequisite for a diplomat. How did Roland get this far? I later found out that he was a "back office" diplomat. His superiors knew his EI was low, so Roland was rarely expected to do the cocktail circuit or participate in face-to-face negotiations with foreign diplomats. His value was in giving expert advice to our negotiators. He had immense knowledge of Soviet culture, language, and history, and he was a brilliant thinker whose cognitive strategies helped conclude an important international treaty. Yet Roland would never lead a diplomatic mission. He had a high IQ but a low EI.

There are many Rolands in the back offices of organizations all over the world. Their cognitive skills are impressive, and they can provide their leaders with alternatives for an important decision, but they seldom become the final decision maker. Numerous research studies support the notion that someone who is not able to incorporate emotional input into decision-making tasks is at a disadvantage when solving problems. For example, Antoine Bechara, Antonio Damasio, and their colleagues at the University of Iowa College of Medicine, compared the responses of normal individuals with those who had brain damage that resulted in very low levels of emotional responding but otherwise normal cognitive function.[8] The researchers used a gambling task to measure decision-making performance, because it simulates real-life decision making by including uncertainty, rewards, and penalties. Skin conductance responses, similar to those used on polygraph machines, measured emotional activity.

Normal participants displayed significant skin conductance responses when making decisions in the gambling task. To the researchers, these responses were evidence of a complex process of unconscious signaling that allows access to previous experiences, specifically those memories shaped by reward, punishment, and the emotional states that accompany them. However, participants with damage to their emotional processing areas failed to notice and incorporate subtle emotional cues into their decision making during the gambling task. Furthermore, they generated no emotional responses when pondering risky choices. Apparently, damage to the emotional response areas in the cortex prevents access to the memories of previous and related decision-making experiences. The researchers concluded that without the help of such memories, a decision maker is at a distinct disadvantage. Our experiences with reward and punishment, sadness and joy, disappointment and success, as well as feelings of pleasure and pain, all produce physiological changes in our body. We feel these changes as distinct emotions that the limbic system encodes as permanent emotional memories.

Components of Emotional Intelligence

Have you ever wondered about your EI? Do you think you have a good understanding of your emotions, and can you use them effectively to your advantage? To help you answer these questions, let's examine the components of EI. Psychologists John Mayer of the University of New Hampshire and Peter Salovey of Yale University conducted extensive studies on the nature of EI that eventually led to a model with four components, ranging from simple to complex abilities.[9] Following are the components, along with twelve statements I constructed from the research that may help you assess your abilities in each area. On a scale of 1 to 5, circle one number per question, with 1 = strongly disagree, 2 = disagree, 3 = neither agree nor disagree, 4 = agree, and 5 = strongly agree.

Ability to perceive and express emotions					
I can easily detect if someone is sad, happy, or disappointed.	1	2	3	4	5
I rarely misinterpret the emotions of others in personal and business situations.	1	2	3	4	5
I easily perceive emotions conveyed by art or music.	1	2	3	4	5
I accurately convey my own emotions to others.	1	2	3	4	5
Ability to assimilate emotions into your thoughts					
I can easily assess the impact that emotions have on my thoughts and decisions.	1	2	3	4	5
I usually integrate emotions into my cognitive thoughts when trying to solve a problem.	1	2	3	4	5
Ability to understand emotions					
I clearly understand how emotions can blend together—for example, that one can be happy and fearful at the same time.	1	2	3	4	5
I clearly understand that emotions can change over time—for example, happiness to boredom, or sadness to anger.	1	2	3	4	5
I can easily understand how certain emotions can isolate me from others and how others can bring relief.	1	2	3	4	5
Ability to effectively manage and regulate emotions					
I am open to emotional experiences when solving problems and making decisions.	1	2	3	4	5
I am effective in managing my own emotions, even in difficult situations.	1	2	3	4	5
I am effective in managing positive and negative emotions in others.	1	2	3	4	5

These questions have not undergone statistical testing for validity, but they can still provide you with some valuable insights. Add up the twelve circled numbers to get a score (maximum of 60). How did you do? A total score between 48 and 60 may indicate that you have a high EI. You could skip the rest of this chapter—unless, of course, you want to learn a few important tips on how to be even better at using your emotions for personal growth and success. Scores below 48 may indicate an average or low EI. If your score is lower than you would like, don't worry; in a bit, we will explore ways in which you can work to raise your EI.

Raising Your Emotional Intelligence

You may be wondering whether a busy executive like yourself should invest the time to consider raising your EI. These research findings on the impact of EI from the Consortium for Research on Emotional Intelligence in Organizations may persuade you:[10]

- Experienced partners in a multinational consulting firm with high EI delivered $1.2 million more profit from their accounts than did other partners with lower EI—a 139 percent incremental gain.

- Research by the Center for Creative Leadership found that the primary reasons given for executives being fired involved deficits in their EI. The three primary causes were difficulty in handling change, not being able to work well in a team, and poor interpersonal relations.

- In a national insurance company, insurance sales agents with a low EI sold policies with an average premium of $54,000. Those who were very strong in EI sold policies worth $114,000.

- A study of 130 executives found that how well people handled their own emotions determined how much people around them preferred to deal with them.

- For sales representatives at a computer company, those hired based on their EI were 90 percent more likely to finish their training than those hired based on other criteria.

- Financial advisers at American Express whose managers completed an EI training program were compared to an equal number whose managers had not. During the year following training, the advisers of trained managers grew their businesses by 18 percent compared to 16 percent for those whose managers were untrained.

And the list goes on.

Four hundred years ago, English philosopher Francis Bacon said, "Knowledge is power." I have heard it hundreds of times, and you probably have, too—but I disagree with the statement. People can have knowledge about something and not act on it or not have it change their behavior. Are you aware of colleagues who *know* better than what they *do*? I sat in a meeting not long ago in which the chairperson spoke nonstop for thirty-five minutes about how important it is to have frequent group participation during a meeting. At the end, those of us who were still awake wondered: "He has the knowledge, but where is the power?" In my opinion, it is much more accurate to say, "The *application* of knowledge is power." If you accept that revision, then you realize that just reading about EI—that is, gaining knowledge of it—will not be enough to master it. To genuinely improve your EI, you must act at the emotional level and engage the emotional parts of your brain as you reflect on your emotions and those of others. Most of what you learn cognitively comes through information that your senses hear, see, and touch. Developing your EI, however, comes through nonverbal and deep sensory learning, as well as practice through real-life interactions with your family, friends, and coworkers.

To keep things simple, psychologist Margaret Chapman says that you can think of the components of EI as falling into two major sets of capabilities, *intrapersonal* and *interpersonal*.[11] Intrapersonal is the portion of EI you use to understand your inner self, including self-awareness, management of emotions and stress, and self-motivation. Interpersonal is the part of EI you use to manage your relationships with others. Let's look first at the intrapersonal capabilities.

> **Gender Differences**
>
> Not surprisingly, researchers studying emotions have reported a few gender differences. Studies indicate that women, compared with men, are more accurate in judging emotional meaning from nonverbal cues, such as one's posture, bearing, and facial expressions. They have more strategies for regulating their emotions and experience their emotions more intensely. Women also show greater emotional awareness and tend to be more empathic than men are. Given these advantages, it is surprising that, despite all the talk of gender equality in business, women account for less than 3 percent of the CEO positions in the 2011 Fortune 500 global list of companies. Obviously, other forces are at work here.

Self-Awareness

One critical element of EI is the ability to see yourself with your own eyes and be aware of your beliefs, your goals, your values, your inner voice, the rules you live by, and the ways these contribute to your perception of the world you live in. You raise your self-awareness when you can provide honest answers to these questions:

- What are your hot buttons—those core beliefs and values, which, if pressed, stir your emotions and spur you into action? Make a list of them, and try to remember the circumstances in which these hot buttons were last pressed. How did you handle it? Would you do the same thing next time?

- How well can you assess the mood of a group during a meeting? At your next meeting, note how people look at each other when speaking or listening. What are their facial expressions? Are they focused, and are they really paying attention to each other's comments, or are they just waiting for their turn to talk? Are there side conversations going on while someone is talking? After the meeting, study your notes and see if you can determine the mood of the group. Were they enthusiastic? Supportive? Cooperative? Clear about what they should do? Such practice helps you use sensory information to make better judgments by moving from what you *think* you see to what you *actually* see.

- How well do you trust your feelings? Are you honest with yourself? For example, suppose a colleague asks you to help her with a project. You already have an overflowing plate, but wanting to be supportive, you agree. She begins to make heavy demands on your time. Now you feel resentment because your original intention (being a helpful coworker) is in conflict with your underlying goal to get your *own* work done. It would have been more honest and less stressful to say no, because that is what you *really* wanted to do.

Management of Emotions and Stress

How well do you manage your emotions and stress? Your biggest enemy in the workplace is worry—the most common emotion among executives. They worry about personnel, clients, time lines, budgets, profit trends, and so on. Worry results in stress, and we already know the toll stress can take on our rational brain and our body. Just managing worry alone can do a great deal to raise your EI and lower your stress level. We do not want to eliminate stress completely. A little stress is healthy, because it helps us stay alert and allows the emotional brain to provide temperate and needed input into our decision making. But situations will always arise that test your reaction to stress.

Consider the following scenario. Late one afternoon, your boss asks you to prepare a report by morning that he can present to the board of directors. It will take hours to gather the data and create the necessary charts. You work at home late into the evening and finish the job. The next morning, your boss is reading the newspaper in his office. You walk in and hand him your completed report. He flips through it, nods, says thanks, lays it down at the corner of his desk, and returns to his paper. Your rational brain is saying, "Guess he liked it or he would have said something." Your emotional brain is pumping up dopamine and going ballistic: "Can you believe that! I worked all night on that report, and all he can say is, 'Thanks'? Not even 'Nice job' or 'It looks great.' What a jerk! Maybe I should go back in there and give him a piece of my mind." What do you do?

Chapman warns that losing your temper may give you some relief, but it is transitory and seldom effective.[12] Too often, it results in significant damage to a professional relationship that is difficult to repair. Furthermore, the outburst raises adrenaline and cortisol levels in your bloodstream—a definite hazard to your health. When faced with a situation like this, it is best to adopt the *six-second rule*: take a deep breath and slowly count to six before you do anything. Six seconds is the time necessary for the prefrontal cortex to rebound from the emotional brain's agitation and reestablish rational control and prevent emotional hijacking. Adopt this technique whenever someone says or does something that triggers your hot button. You will be surprised how well it works. After you calm down, ask yourself these questions:

- How am I interpreting what just happened?
- What evidence do I have to support my interpretation?
- What do I have to lose and gain if I say or do this?
- What will I learn if I do or do not say or do this?
- What is the worst that can happen?

Write down what specific steps you will take if the worst possible outcome occurs. Be methodical and realistic. If the worst happens, follow your plan. If not, be thankful, remember the lesson, and move on.

Self-Motivation

Another important aspect of EI is the ability to communicate with yourself. Now let me explain before you get uneasy and think that this is going to be touchy-feely chatter of questionable value. For years, valid psychological studies have shown the power of psychosomatic connections—that is, the control that the mind can exert over your behavior and well-being. In many instances, the body will do only what the mind believes it can do. Consequently, self-talk can be a vigorous motivator for good and a useful weapon to fend off any anxiety about an upcoming decision. Starting each day with a positive attitude and belief in yourself can go a long way in motivating you to meet the day's challenges.

To prove the power of psychosomatic connections, I often do the following group activity. I convince a strong-looking man to come to the front of the room, and I ask him to extend his arm out to his side. I tell him that I am going to push his arm back down to his side and ask him to resist me with all his power. Then I ask him to think of some activity that he does poorly and to keep repeating in his head, "I am really bad at that," while I push down on his arm. Invariably, despite his resistance, I succeed. The negative self-talk literally saps his strength! Then I ask him to think of some activity he does very well and to keep repeating in his head, "I am really terrific at that," while I push down on his arm. I usually lose because the positive self-talk has revved up his energy enough to resist me.

Another aspect of self-motivation, Chapman suggests, is building an A-team, whereby you surround yourself with trusted colleagues, associates, and friends who can provide you with different types of support both at and away from work.[13] These people can be valuable assets when your self-motivation sags and needs recharging. Make a list of those people:

- Who make you feel valued as a coworker and friend
- On whom you can depend in a crisis
- Who can give you honest feedback about your work
- Who introduce you to new people, new ideas, and new interests
- With whom you can share bad news
- With whom you can share good news and good feelings
- Who are always a valuable and reliable source of information

Now let's look at the interpersonal capabilities of EI—those that describe your emotional responses to the behavior and emotions of others. You can also use your EI capabilities to help make others aware of their own EI behaviors.

Relationships With Others in the Workplace

Leadership consultant Roger Pearman suggests that you enhance your EI when you exhibit certain emotion-related behaviors in workplace situations.[14] For example, how would you use EI to manage an unmotivated employee? The high-EI method would be to enter into empathetic discussions with the employee to discover what underlying needs the work environment is not meeting. Exploring stress-coping strategies could also help build the employee's own EI capabilities.

How would you deal with an unhappy client? Listening with an empathetic ear to the client's concerns is a good start. Former Secretary of State Dean Rusk once said, "One of the best ways to persuade people is with your ears—by listening to them." Engage the individual, and be constructive and optimistic in telling the client that you will use your problem-solving skills to produce better customer satisfaction. What about helping a team leader who is ineffective? Find out whether the leader needs help with interpersonal skills, such as developing greater flexibility, and determine what EI strategies will boost the team leader's effectiveness.

A genuine test of your EI comes when there is a major change under way in your workplace for which you need to implement the initiatives necessary for that change to occur. Have you ever been in this situation? How did you deal with it? If you have a high EI, you know how important it is to be empathetic to the concerns of others regarding the changes. It is no secret that human beings generally do not like change. That may be because in our cave ancestors' days, change always meant disaster in some form: flood, fire, famine, insect invasion, and so on. Our memory system learned to associate change with an undesirable event, and that deep-rooted association is still present in our genetic predispositions. Consequently, change causes stress. The high-EI executive who shows tolerance for the stress embedded in the situation and who remains optimistic about the future will be more likely to lead change effectively.

Like most executives, you probably spend more time in the workplace and meeting with clients after office hours than you do with your family and friends. Relationships with colleagues and clients become a significant contributor to your mental well-being. Sour workplace relationships can increase stress to dangerous levels, whereas tranquil relationships can enhance your effectiveness and overall happiness. Chapman suggests that executives can build strong, healthy relationships with colleagues when they allow their emotional brain to direct certain behaviors.[15] Ask yourself how you would rank yourself for each of the following statements by circling 1 for low, 2 for medium, and 3 for high. When you are done, decide how you want to address any areas for which you circled a 1. It is not difficult to find executives who can develop mission statements, read profit-and-loss statements, and analyze data. It is much tougher to find executives who truly understand that organizations are run by people and who have the ability to build productive relationships. That is the essence of emotional intelligence.

Statement	Low	Medium	High
I show my appreciation for the individual skills, knowledge, and capabilities of my colleagues.	1	2	3
I make time to get to know my colleagues and listen empathetically to what they have to say.	1	2	3
I support my colleagues whenever they have tough times.	1	2	3
I make it a point to spend social time with my colleagues.	1	2	3
I give positive feedback to my colleagues for a job well done.	1	2	3
I seek the advice and opinions of my colleagues whenever I can.	1	2	3
I establish a positive emotional climate, including common courtesies and friendly greetings, whenever I meet with my colleagues in a group.	1	2	3
Whenever I have a disagreement with a colleague, I look for an early and just solution.	1	2	3

Handling the Emotions of a Crisis

Leaders with high EI recognize the importance of dealing with the emotional turmoil that erupts when a crisis occurs in an organization. Whether it is a major accident or an act of employee violence, you need to be there to calm fears, provide solace, and show that you are focusing on solving any issues. The importance of this became clear to me on a sunny Thursday morning in London.

It was July 7, 2005. I had been invited to present a one-day seminar at a weeklong conference in the Tower Hotel, just across the street from the daunting Tower of London and the impressive Tower Bridge. More than sixty participants had signed up for my session, which was to begin at 9:30 a.m. Coffee, tea, and light refreshments were ready by 8:30 a.m., and a few people started drifting in. I was setting up my materials, greeting the arrivals, and looking forward to an exciting day. I certainly got some excitement, but it was not what I expected.

At 8:50 that morning, suicide attackers exploded three bombs within fifty seconds of each other in the London Underground. One of the lines hit by an explosion ran to Aldgate, just a few blocks from our hotel. An hour later, a fourth bomb exploded on a double-decker bus in Tavistock Square. In all, the explosions killed fifty-six people, including the four terrorists, and injured about seven hundred. It was the deadliest bombing in London since World War II. The timing of the explosions left Londoners wondering whether more bombs would detonate. Rumors were running rampant, and the city desperately needed reassurance.

Prime Minister Tony Blair was at the G8 summit in Scotland, where he delivered a brief but powerful statement, reminding Londoners:

> Those engaged in terrorism realize that our determination to defend our values and our way of life is greater than their determination to cause death and destruction to innocent people in a desire to impose extremism on the world. Whatever they do, it is our determination that they will never succeed in destroying what we hold dear in this country and other civilized nations throughout the world.[16]

He left the G8 meeting immediately and returned to London, where he toured the bombing sites, reassured the public on radio and television, and expressed gratitude for the heroic work of the emergency services. A strong leader made a strong statement, both in words and by his very presence.

When a crisis occurs in your organization, you need to be there—pronto! If the crisis happens in more than one location, then send out your senior management team to the various sites. Be sure to offer words of encouragement and assurances that all issues are being addressed. Talk to individuals, remembering that it is the workers who make the organization run; they need this emotional support in times of organizational distress. Your colleagues may not remember much of what you say, but they will remember that you were there and that you recognized the importance of their work. Blair made sure he visited the firehouses, police stations, and hospitals. He knew the importance of talking to the rescue workers and thanking them for the risks they took amid the uncertainty of other explosions.

As for my seminar, thirty-five people eventually showed up. One man came in around ten o'clock with patches of soot on his hands and clothing. He apologized for his appearance and joined the others as though nothing had happened. A few minutes later, a woman arrived, still bleeding slightly from her nose. She said she fell on the stairs in the Underground as people were rushing out to escape the smoke. I asked if she needed medical help. "No, thank you," she said in a calm voice. "I'll just go off to the ladies' room for a minute to clean up." She returned and was an active participant the rest of the day. Personally, I was stunned by the resilience and determination of these Londoners. They obviously took Tony Blair's emotional message to heart and went on with their lives—a prime example of resiliency.

Mindfulness and Resiliency

Have you ever suffered a major failure? If not, count your blessings, but be prepared, because one is coming. Whether it is failing in a marriage, losing a job, or having a good decision yield unexpectedly bad outcomes, failure is part of life. The important thing is how you respond to it. After an extreme adversity, some people fall apart, get depressed, and never recover. Most people get depressed at first but eventually bounce back to normal functioning—a characteristic known as *resilience*. A few get depressed but somehow end up stronger than they were before the trauma. Why the different outcomes? Psychologist Martin Seligman at the University of Pennsylvania claims the difference is optimism.[17] Known as the father of positive psychology, Seligman says that those who interpret a setback as temporary and who are convinced that they can do something about it are less likely to get depressed or give up after failure. In effect, their optimism inoculates them against the worst aftereffects of a trauma. Although this approach can work well for the rare major failures, dealing with the more frequent daily setbacks and annoying disappointments requires a more disciplined approach.

Brain scans reveal that when we are distressed over an upsetting incident, the right prefrontal cortex is highly active. As we recover, the left prefrontal areas become active and the right regions quiet down. Right-side active—we are stressed out; left-side active—we demonstrate resilience. Therefore, researchers concluded that training the brain to focus calmly on the problem could give the left-side brain regions time to help us recover from the stress and anxiety caused by the problem, rather than reacting to it while in a disturbed state. In other words, quiet reflection can enhance our resilience.

One research-based approach for enhancing resilience is *mindfulness*, a form of meditation that teaches the brain to focus one's complete attention on an immediate experience without reacting to it. The idea is to get the details from the upsetting event out of working memory so your stress and anxiety can subside and to shift your focus to an internal process, such as your breathing.

The procedure is really quite simple. You will need a quiet and private place where you can be undistracted for a few minutes. If it is your office, be sure to turn off your phones and email. Sit up comfortably, and focus on your breathing, keeping your attention on the feelings of inhaling and exhaling. Make no judgments about your breathing, and do not change it in any way. If other thoughts or distractions come to mind, dismiss them and focus again on your breathing. Just as you set a routine for physical exercise, do the same for this mental exercise by setting aside about twenty minutes a day for mindfulness. It will help build those brain circuits that manage resiliency.

Empathy: I Feel Your Pain

Because we are social animals, the human brain is primed to respond to the joy and sadness of others, setting off neural systems that generate similar feelings within ourselves. In essence, we can feel someone else's pain. Displaying sincere empathy tells others that you care about them as individual human beings, not just as workers. Take the story of James Allen Ward, who was a swashbuckling twenty-two-year-old sergeant in the Royal New Zealand Air Force. In July 1941, he was the copilot of a Wellington bomber flying 13,000 feet over the North Sea on a bombing raid when a German fighter attacked his plane. The attack opened a fuel tank on the starboard wing, and the engine caught fire. Realizing the plane was doomed, the crew prepared to bail out, despite the danger of the German warplane shooting at their parachutes in midair. But the plane's skipper told the crew to wait while Ward crawled out onto the wing with a rope tied around his waist, inched his way toward the engine, and smothered the fire with a piece of canvas. He crawled back into the cockpit, and the plane and its entire crew landed safely in England.

Ward was awarded the Victoria Cross, Britain's highest military honor, for his bravery. Word of his exploits got to Winston Churchill, who invited Ward to 10 Downing Street to congratulate him on this feat. Despite his fearlessness, the aviator was dumbfounded in the presence of the prime minister and had difficulty responding to questions. Churchill sensed his visitor's discomfort and said, "You must feel very humble and awkward in my presence." "Yes, sir," replied

Ward. "I do." Churchill said, "Then you can imagine how humble and awkward I feel in yours."[18] What a stunning display of empathy from the leader of a nation at war.

Regardless of your position in the organization, an empathetic style will always serve you well. It convinces colleagues of your best intentions and increases their loyalty to you and the organization.

A Final Word About the Emotional Brain

Perhaps by now you recognize the importance of respecting the contributions from your emotional brain when making decisions in the workplace and in your personal life. That emotional input is an evolutionary artifact that allows for a blend of cognitive thinking tempered with a spirit that pervades everything you do. It helps you get back in touch with those personal values that really matter. The emotional brain often knows better. It certainly did in my case. Remember that big career decision I discussed at the beginning of the chapter? I quit that job and never looked back.

Emotions aside, major decisions usually require a considerable amount of thinking. Your brain needs to acquire information, then analyze and evaluate options with the intent of formulating possible solutions. How you go about doing all this is partially influenced by your genetic makeup, but more largely the result of whatever system you used when solving problems in the past. Was your process thorough or haphazard? Did you get enough information? Did you consider the consequences of your decision? Recently, scientists have been reexamining some of the long-standing ideas about thinking and are especially interested in answering this question: Can we actually teach ourselves to improve our thinking skills? Find out the answer to this intriguing question in the next chapter.

CHAPTER FOUR

Improving Your Thinking

We cannot solve our problems with the same thinking we used when we created them.

ALBERT EINSTEIN

A FEW YEARS AGO, THE NATIONAL SCIENCE FOUNDATION ESTIMATED THAT the average human brain generates between 12,000 and 50,000 thoughts per day, depending on how deep a thinker the person is. The unsettling part of this statistic is that most of these thoughts are nonsense—lamenting over the past, combating guilt, worrying about the future, drifting into fantasy, and playing with fiction. Frequently, these thoughts are negative, wasting valuable neural energy on past and unchangeable events. This leaves just a few thoughts for positive and consequential things. Being mindful of your thoughts is another important step toward raising your emotional intelligence and a key factor in getting the most from your brain's extraordinary capabilities.

Thinking is essential to your survival and to your success as a leader. Do you ever think about your thinking? Ever wonder how a three-pound mass of tangible flesh can create such phantom things like ideas? Or how electric signals traveling across tiny cells can produce a symphony, design a computer, or create a weapon of mass destruction? From birth (some say, before), the brain collects information about the world and organizes it to form a representation of that world. This mental model describes thinking, the process we use to function in our environment.

Thinking includes daily routines, such as knowing where we are now, where we want to be, and how to get there. Other aspects of thinking center on concept development, creativity, logic, learning, memory, and communication. For example, the brain uses logic to recognize that if A is equal to B, and B is equal to C, then A must be equal to C. Other thinking mechanisms include identifying patterns, constructing mental images, and approximating. How well we use these aspects often determines whether we have success or failure in our interactions with the environment and with others.

Some types of thinking require more mental effort than other types. Let's rev up your brain by getting you to think about the answers to these questions:

- Who was the first president of the United States?
- What are the similarities and differences between the US involvement in the wars in Vietnam and Iraq?
- Defend why we should or should not have the death penalty for certain crimes.

How did you do? Did you find your brain working harder as you moved through the questions? The type of thinking involved in answering these three questions varies. Just the effortless recall of a fact from long-term memory will answer the first question. The second question requires more mental effort. You must first recall what you remember about both wars, separate those facts into lists, and then determine which items are similar and which are different. Answering the third question is harder still. You will need to review and process all you know about the death penalty, its impact on society, its effectiveness as a deterrent to crime, and the implications of how recent DNA evidence has exonerated persons the legal system has already executed. Then you need to form a judgment about whether you believe the death penalty will influence a criminal's behavior. Clearly, these three questions require increasingly complex thought processes for you to arrive at acceptable answers.

Higher-order thinking requires using cognitive mechanisms that have multiple networks designed to provide a solution with great accuracy. However, these mechanisms are slow and require considerable attentiveness. They may also interfere with other cognitive tasks you wish to perform. Other less accurate mechanisms, however, are fast, involve little attentiveness, and do not interfere with other tasks. Consequently, when faced with a problem, we tend to use the cognitive processing system that requires the least amount of effort, even if it is less accurate. Here is a problem that will demonstrate this process. Try to answer before reading ahead.

> Adam is texting Stacey, but Stacey is texting Rick. Adam is a minor, but Rick is not. Is a minor texting an adult? (A) Yes, (B) No, (C) Cannot be determined

Is your answer C? Most people choose C because they quickly assume they cannot solve the problem without knowing whether Stacey is a minor or an adult. However, consider both possibilities for Stacey. If she is an adult, the answer is A, because Adam (a minor) is texting her. If Stacey is a minor, the answer is still A, because she is texting Rick, who is an adult. If you answered C, your brain defaulted to the simplest inference without thinking through all the possibilities. Here is a chance to try again.

> A fancy shirt and a tie cost $55.00 in total. The shirt costs $50 more than the tie. How much does the tie cost?

Most people will quickly do a simple mental subtraction and say that the tie costs $5.00. This is wrong, because then the shirt would have to cost $55.00, for a total cost of $60.00. The tie costs $2.50.

Fret not. Large numbers of students at Ivy League colleges have given incorrect answers to problems like these. The lesson you should learn here is that your brain tends to take the easy way out when solving problems, often leading to incorrect and illogical answers. Quiz shows and timed tests have led us to believe that speed of response is the mark of high intelligence and powerful thinking. However, slow and deliberate processing more often leads to the correct answer. Just slow down and think about your thinking.

Metacognition

Many animals think, but as far as we know, humans are the only creatures who can think *about* their thinking. This is *metacognition*. The human brain is so incredible that it can contemplate itself. Because thinking is so important to your success, you are going to have the opportunity in this chapter to explore the various ways you think. Armed with that information, you may want to consider improving some of your thinking skills so you can be even more successful at what you do. Yes, you read that correctly: you *can* improve your thinking skills! The brain is continually expanding and reorganizing neural networks in response to its environment. Like many skills, practice improves performance. By practicing complex thinking patterns, you can improve your ability to acquire, understand, apply, analyze, and evaluate information, as well as create new ideas. Why does this matter? Because thinking about how you arrived at a decision may help you avoid errors in the future.

We are going to start by considering your basic thinking style preference. Thinking style preference? What's that? For decades, psychologists have examined the various ways people approach problem solving and decision making. Researchers have developed numerous models and questionnaires, the Myers-Briggs Type Indicator being one of the more popular commercial ones. Completing such a questionnaire is intended to reveal the preferred habits of mind that construct your view of the world, how it works, and how you see yourself in it. This is helpful information because it tends to reveal how you really interact with your world rather than how you think you interact with it. It also helps you understand the thinking preferences of others, useful information if you want to include people who think differently from you in your decision-making process.

Logical and Holistic Thinking Preferences

One long-standing noncommercial thinking preferences model is simple yet revealing. It stems from years of research on the notion that specific regions of the brain process certain thinking and personality preferences. This model looks at two general thinking preferences: logical and holistic. Years ago, these terms were associated with different hemispheres of the brain—the left hemisphere being considered as the logical region and the right hemisphere as the holistic area. Perhaps you remember hearing pop culture expressions such as, "She's very left-brained" or "He's an artist—very right-brained." However, recent brain imaging studies show that although these left-logical/right-holistic associations do seem valid, they are a lot weaker than brain researchers first thought. The cerebral hemispheres constantly communicate with each other through a thick cable in the center of the brain called the *corpus callosum*. Their degree of communication varies with the task, but it is very rare for only one hemisphere to be principally involved in any complex problem-solving or decision-making activity. Nonetheless, the logical–holistic dichotomy is a useful tool for assessing thinking preferences. Let's look at each one further.

Logical Thinking Preference

Individuals with a predominantly logical thinking preference are analytical and evaluate factual material in a rational, detached way. They are good at arithmetic and solving sequential problems. They focus on the literal interpretation of words and are sensitive to time units and sequence. They seek coherent explanations for why events occur and are very good at expressing themselves in reasoned rather than emotional language.

Holistic Thinking Preference

Those with a predominantly holistic thinking preference are highly intuitive. They are good at spatial mathematics and solving open-ended problems. They paint and draw well and deal with the visual world more easily than the verbal one. As a result, they gather more information from images than from words, and they probe for patterns. They interpret what people say more through context—body language, emotional content, and tone of voice—than through literal meanings.

Thinking Preferences Are Not Exclusive

Researchers in this area emphasize that an individual's thinking preference tends to be more predominant during complex processing and that this preference affects personality, abilities, and how we learn. Using this model, the individual's thinking preference runs the gamut from neutral (no preference) to a strongly logical or holistic preference. A moderate to strong preference for either type of thinking does not mean that we do not use both types when the occasion calls for it. In doing a simple task, we use the thinking component that will help us accomplish the task more efficiently. When we are faced with a task that is more complex, however, our personal thinking preference will often take the lead, although characteristics of the nonpreferred thinking type will almost certainly get involved as well. Thus, our thinking process benefits from the integration of the processing done by multiple brain areas, and we are afforded greater comprehension of whatever situation started the processing.

Assessing Your Logical/Holistic Thinking Preference

There are many questionnaires available to assess your logical/holistic thinking preference. The tool provided here takes just a few minutes and will give you an indication of your preference. The results are not conclusive, so if this is an area of particular interest, you may want to seek out additional questionnaires to collect more data before reaching any firm conclusion about your logical/holistic thinking preference.

Directions: From each pair below, mark A or B corresponding to the sentence that best describes you. Do not spend too much time with any one question. Your first response is usually the most accurate. Answer all questions. There are no right or wrong answers.

1.	A. I prefer to find my own way of doing a new task. B. I prefer to be told the best way to do a new task.	
2.	A. I have to make my own plans. B. I can follow anyone's plans.	
3.	A. I am a very flexible and occasionally unpredictable person. B. I am a very stable and consistent person.	
4.	A. I keep everything in a particular place. B. Where I keep things depends on what I am doing.	
5.	A. I spread my work evenly over the time I have. B. I prefer to do my work at the last minute.	
6.	A. I know I am right because I have good reasons. B. I know when I am right, even without reasons.	
7.	A. I need a lot of variety and change in my life. B. I need a well-planned and orderly life.	
8.	A. I sometimes have too many ideas in a new situation. B. I sometimes don't have any ideas in a new situation.	
9.	A. I do easy things first and the important things last. B. I do the important things first and the easy things last.	
10.	A. I choose what I know is right when making a hard decision. B. I choose what I feel is right when making a hard decision.	
11.	A. I plan my time for doing my work. B. I don't think about the time when I work.	
12.	A. I usually have good self-discipline. B. I usually act on my feelings.	
13.	A. Other people don't understand how I organize things. B. Other people think I organize things well.	
14.	A. I agree with new ideas before other people do. B. I question new ideas more than other people do.	
15.	A. I tend to think more in pictures. B. I tend to think more in words.	
16.	A. I try to find the one best way to solve a problem. B. I try to find different ways to solve a problem.	
17.	A. I can usually analyze what is going to happen next. B. I can usually sense what is going to happen next.	

18.	A. I am not very imaginative in my work. B. I use my imagination in nearly everything I do.	
19.	A. I begin many jobs that I never finish. B. I finish a job before starting a new one.	
20.	A. I look for new ways to do old jobs. B. When one way works well, I don't change it.	
21.	A. It is fun to take risks. B. I have fun without taking risks.	

Interpreting Your Score: Count the number of A and B responses to the following questions to determine your thinking style preference.

Count the number of A responses to questions 1, 3, 7, 8, 9, 13, 14, 15, 19, 20, and 21.

Place that number on the line to the right.   A:_____

Count the number of B responses to the remaining questions.

Place that number on the line to the right.   B:_____

Total the A and B responses.   Total:_____

The total indicates your logical/holistic preference according to the following scale.

0-5	Strong logical thinking preference
6-8	Moderate logical thinking preference
9-12	Balance (little or no thinking preference)
13-15	Moderate holistic thinking preference
16-21	Strong holistic thinking preference

Did your score surprise you? Why or why not? What does your score tell you about your approach to decision making? Logical/holistic thinking preferences affect your personality, view of the world, and interaction with others, as well as the methods you use to make presentations in meetings. People whose logical/holistic thinking preference is similar to yours are more likely to find you easy to understand and work with. Conversely, those whose thinking preference is considerably different from yours will have difficulty understanding your views or approaches to problem solving and decision making.

Managers and Leaders

Some researchers suggest that people with a strong logical thinking preference make excellent managers because of their strengths in logic and analysis. Managers do things right. They are strong on organization and procedures, produce highly detailed job descriptions, and generally run a tight ship. However, such a formal organization can be devoid of empathy and be overly protective. Some people who work in this setting might not be motivated because there is no esprit de corps in the organization, and some might feel underappreciated, like they are just putting in the hours in an impersonal establishment.

On the other hand, individuals with a holistic thinking preference tend to make more effective leaders for change. Leaders do the right thing. They tend to run looser organizations in which people work toward a common vision and feel valued for what they do. Effective leaders often have to think outside the box, persuade reluctant people, and find creative solutions to old problems. People with a strongly holistic thinking preference usually possess the charisma, empathy, and imagination to be successful in a leadership role, even though they often feel overwhelmed by bureaucracy and details. However, some people working for this type of a leader might sense a lack of direction and feel uncertain about their job expectations.

Many people possess the qualities of both logical and holistic thinking preferences to some degree, but few excel in both. What if you just found out that you have a strong logical thinking preference but are now in a position of leadership? Are you doomed? Is this a mismatch destined for failure? Probably not. Obviously, you have talents, skills, and a record of accomplishments that have gotten you this far. Nonetheless, you might want to work on raising your EI to develop the skills of empathy and creativity that encourage others to accept your leadership, especially when you need to bring about change.

Managing a company today is a tough job; leading one is even tougher. Leaders need to be creative, ethical, inspiring, and respectful, as well as knowledgeable about the law, methods of informing others, and social and cultural institutions. They have to articulate a clear vision to their colleagues. They should know how to identify and support areas that enhance the mission of the organization and modify those areas that impede it. If leaders are made and not born, how can you acquire the skills needed to be a leader and not just a manager? How will you use these skills to implement change? In the next sections, we identify specific cognitive forces and personal habits of mind and explore how they interact when you bring change to the workplace.

Cognitive Forces and Decision Making

Based on current neuroscience, I suggest that people in positions of true leadership—those who see themselves primarily as change agents—are subject to the following major cerebral forces influencing their thinking and behavior: creativity, stability, relationships, results, and purpose. After you read the description of each, rate yourself on a scale of 1 to 5.

Creativity

Creativity describes your tendency to seek out alternatives for solving problems and taking actions that contribute to survival, quality of life, and excellent performance at your job. This force helps you explore options, think outside the box, support change, and clarify the vision of where to go next and in the future. It also embraces the notion of putting together ideas in new and different ways that are persuasive to others. You always ask yourself, "What's a novel way to introduce this concept to the other members of this organization so they will buy into it?" We will dig further into creativity later in this chapter.

Your creativity score:

Little	Average	High
1	2	3	4	5

Stability

Stability refers to your tendency to retain and protect activities that bring stability, certainty, order, and logic to daily situations. This force helps you keep control over those resources that maintain balance and allow for a calm existence within the organization. The reality that most humans do not take well to change attests to the power of this force. You always wonder, "Will what I am contemplating bring about too much change at one time?"

Your stability score:

Little	Average	High
1	2	3	4	5

Relationships

Relationships explain how consistently you seek out linkages and connections to others and avoid taking actions that undermine those relationships. This force encourages you to rely on the loyalty and commitment of others to support your initiatives. As a leader, you are always thinking, "Am I alienating too many close colleagues with this decision?"

Your relationships score:

Little	Average	High
1	2	3	4	5

Results

Results refers to your tendency to get things done and feel the satisfaction of accomplishment. This force enhances the positive feelings that come with closure. It makes you think, "We have been talking about this for years. Now we can make it happen."

Your results score:

Little	Average	High
1	2	3	4	5

Purpose

Purpose describes your tendency to justify any and all workplace actions as being consistent with the organization's purpose, vision, and mission. This force tends to integrate all the other forces to help you arrive at a final decision. You are always saying, "With this decision, we come closer to fulfilling our firm's mission."

Your purpose score:

Little	Average	High
1	2	3	4	5

Now, review your scores. It is unusual for someone in a leadership position to have all 1s. If you do, count your blessings and do not tell a soul! It is also unusual to get all 5s because several of these forces are independent but complementary parts of your cerebral processing system, and they vary in intensity. They can act together in various combinations or in opposition, depending on the situation. How each force influences a given situation often determines what skills and information you need to solve a problem or handle conflict. Here is an example of how these forces interact.

Faced with the deteriorating effectiveness of a colleague who is also a close personal friend, you might avoid discussing poor job performance for fear of damaging your long-standing friendship. In this case, the relationship force, based primarily in the emotional area of the brain, wields greater influence than the prefrontal-cortex-based results and stability forces that seek to maintain work productivity. If your colleague's performance worsens, you could use the creativity force to design strategies that support the colleague in positive ways, thus lessening the chance that such action would adversely affect your personal relationship. Nonetheless, if performance still does not improve, then the purpose force should ultimately prevail. At that point, you would need to counsel your friend to find a way to leave the organization.

Personal Habits of Mind

The brain directs and controls the many different functions that affect how we think, decide, and act. Thus, our thinking and learning preferences, creativity, intelligence, and personality traits enhance or hinder the influence of the cerebral forces just described. People who are gregarious and strong in interpersonal intelligence, for instance, are likely to be more influenced by the relationships force. Those who are stronger in logic might be influenced more by the stability force. Other important thinking preference differences also exist and are often referred to as *habits of mind*. Once again, you can rate yourself on the major habits by circling the choice that best describes you for each characteristic *most* of the time. There are no right or wrong answers, only revealing ones.

Collaboration

When gathering information or solving problems, do you prefer high, moderate, or little collaboration with others, or do you prefer to gather information and process it alone?

High collaboration	Moderate collaboration
Little collaboration	Alone

Evaluation of Relevant Information

Do you tend to evaluate relevant information based on logic and analysis, or do you rely more on emotions and values to guide your decision?

More logic/analysis	Some logic/analysis
Some emotion/values	More emotion/values

Experiences

We also experience the world differently. Do you prefer an abstract approach—that is, collecting experiences through books, videos, and discussions? Or do you prefer a more concrete approach—that is, interacting directly with people and your environment and getting firsthand experiences?

Mostly abstract	Some abstract
Some concrete	Mostly concrete

Speed of Decision Making

Do you prefer to make decisions quickly, regardless of the issue, or do you prefer a deliberate, well-thought-out process, no matter the urgency?

Speed first	Some speed
Some deliberation	Mostly deliberation

Perspective

Do you tend to focus primarily on details, data, and sequence, or do you prefer to look more at relationships that form the big picture?

Mostly on details/data	Some on details/data
Some on relationships	Mostly on relationships

Review the choices you circled; these responses give you additional insights into your thinking processes. Whenever you make decisions, all these cerebral forces and habits of mind are at hand, subconsciously directing which skills are brought into play and influencing what information you use or ignore. By being aware of these forces and the role each one plays, as well as your own thinking preferences, you are more apt to make decisions that are supportive of your organization's mission as you work to bring about effective change.

Creativity and Change

Problems facing complex organizations are seldom easy to fix because there rarely is a single solution. Is this the time to expand into international markets? Is it time to issue more stock? What is the most cost-effective way to increase production? How do we downsize without seriously damaging worker morale? Most likely, several solutions to each problem exist, each with its own list of advantages and disadvantages. These types of problems require creative approaches, and the company CEO needs to have a menu of plausible suggestions. In other words, the more creative an executive you are, the higher the likelihood you can meet the expectations of your job.

Can I Improve My Creativity?

We need to clarify that creativity is different from intelligence. Numerous studies have shown that these two capabilities are not interrelated, and a high score on one does not predict a high score on the other. Brain scan images indicate that the brain treats creativity and intelligence as separate abilities and recruits from different areas when solving complex problems. These findings confirm what many of us have already observed: smart people are not always creative, and creative people are not always smart.

For many years, psychologists thought that creativity, like intelligence, was a fixed innate ability—either you were born with it, or you were not. Of course, once you accept the idea of creativity (or intelligence) as a single immutable trait, then there is no sense in trying to change it. However, our understanding of creativity has evolved, just as it has for intelligence. Researchers now see these entities as multidimensional, fluid, and mutable. Human creative potential can be cultivated and developed. There are, no doubt, genetically encoded limits, but they are much broader and weaker than we once thought. Starting with this growth-oriented mindset, researchers began studies designed to determine whether people could improve their creativity. The results: people can, indeed, learn and enhance aspects of their creativity. Furthermore, the studies revealed little or no difference in creativity scores between males and females.

Impediments to Being Creative

Before we begin exploring how to improve creativity, we need to identify and remove some common blocks to creativity, which include the following:

- **Routines**. The "we've always done it this way" approach to solving problems may be useful at times, but it can limit the range of options available to you when you are seeking creative solutions. Shake up those routines that impede progress toward your goal.

- **Stress**. A little stress is good in that it keeps you active, but too much stress drains neural and physical energy that you could otherwise use to develop creative options. Manage your stress. See chapter 5 for suggestions on how to do that.

- **Beliefs**. Strongly held beliefs can sometimes be ports in a storm, but they can also limit the way you see the world by filtering out information that contradicts your beliefs. Through such filtering, you lose awareness of other options. Having beliefs is fine, as long as you recognize that all beliefs have limitations and do not allow them to prevent you from looking at other possibilities. In some cases, consider defending a position that is very different from your own just to become familiar with its content and to gain an understanding of why others may hold that belief.

- **Ego**. There are several components to this block. One is fear of the judgments that others might make about your proposals. Not all of them may be flattering, a potential blow to your ego. Other components include being overly self-critical about your work ("This just isn't perfect!") and being too wrapped up in negative thinking ("I'm really not able to do this!").

Strategies for Improving Creativity

Generating creative solutions to complex problems requires opening up your long-term memory so that all relevant and even marginally relevant information you already possess is available for active manipulation. This process requires significant mental resources and energy and can be very tiring. The human brain is effective but not efficient. Although it represents about 2 percent of our body weight, it consumes more than 20 percent of our calories.

Michael Arrigo, an associate professor of art at Bowling Green State University, has some definite ideas about how we can improve our creativity.[1] When your creative thinking feels sluggish, try some of these strategies to recharge and support your neural systems and give your creativity a little boost:

- **List the attributes of the problem**. Make a list of all the attributes you can think of that relate to the problem at hand. Here is a simple problem we can use as an example. Say you are looking for a better way to review the unexpectedly large number of résumés your office now receives for each job opening. Write down as many attributes of the process as possible. The more detailed the list, the greater value it is to the creative process. For instance, the review process should be time efficient, it should be labor efficient, it should be thorough so as not to miss potentially good candidates, it should be completed in-house, and so on. Study the attributes and see if they give you any new insights.

- **List things you do not like about the problem**. You might list, for example, that the organization does not give specific directions on what to include in résumés, there is no limit to the number of pages, there is not sufficient in-house staff to do a timely review, and so on.

- **Reverse the problem**. Instead of thinking about ways to solve the problem, think of those things that could make the problem worse. As bizarre as this might sound, problem reversal can sometimes give you insights into a potential solution that you might not otherwise consider. In our sample problem, this would involve considering everything that would make the résumé-screening process more cumbersome and inefficient, such as waiting until the deadline date before opening any of the envelopes or calling a meeting of the review committee to read all the résumés at one sitting.

- **Question your assumptions**. Review the problem and decide which assumptions are worth questioning and which battles are worth fighting. For example: Why do we assume that we need résumés at all? Instead of dealing with all that paperwork, why not contact a few key people who could recommend potential candidates?

- **Change your perspective**. The environment in which you work influences your thinking. When you enter your office, your brain shifts into routine thinking patterns that get you through your day. Different environments trigger other thinking patterns. With this strategy, you think about the problem in a very different environment. Perhaps the creative solution to screening résumés efficiently will come to you during a walk near your home, in the hardware store, in the supermarket, or in the shower.

- **Assume you are wrong**. At first look, this may seem like self-criticism, which we already identified as a block to creativity, but on closer inspection, this strategy forces you to test your own solution and pushes you to look again at alternative solutions. It causes you to think about the information you may not want to think about and give some attention to data that challenge your beliefs. Often you will find that no one solution is completely satisfactory, so this process encourages you to look for variations and compromises.

These strategies do work. Just ask Elena Karpova and her colleagues at Iowa State University.[2] They tested a broad sample of 114 university students for creativity using the widely recognized Torrance Test of Creative Thinking (TTCT). As part of their regular classes, the students received instruction in creativity strategies, similar to those just described. They learned and practiced the strategies for a period of eight to twelve weeks. After a retest, a large majority of the students showed significant gains in their creativity scores.

Here is another research finding worth a moment of your time. If you have been employed for several decades or longer, practicing these creativity strategies becomes more urgent. Research studies show that our creativity levels drop the longer we are in the workplace. Faye McIntyre, an associate professor of marketing at the State University of West Georgia, and her colleagues discovered that the creativity scores (as measured by the TTCT) of marketing students in graduate school declined the longer they were employed.[3] Although it is not possible to say for certain what causes this decline, one plausible explanation is that the longer individuals remain in a job, the more routine their thinking becomes, thus deterring, rather than enhancing, creative abilities.

A Final Word About Thinking Skills

The good news is that, regardless of your age, you *can* improve your thinking skills and your creativity. However, it takes determination, motivation, and practice. The best way to be creative is to be creative!

Now let us look at how you can use this information to make you and your colleagues more successful in the workplace.

CHAPTER FIVE

Leading by Dissent

I not only use all the brains that I have,
but all that I can borrow.

WOODROW WILSON

Iɴ Mᴀʀᴄʜ 2011, ɪɴᴛᴇʟʟɪɢᴇɴᴄᴇ ᴇxᴘᴇʀᴛꜱ ᴛᴏʟᴅ Pʀᴇsɪᴅᴇɴᴛ Oʙᴀᴍᴀ ᴛʜᴀᴛ, after their extensive analysis of evidence collected over an eight-month period, chances were better than fifty-fifty that Osama bin Laden was living in a three-story compound in Abbottabad, Pakistan. The president's dilemma: how to capture or kill bin Laden without alerting the occupants of the compound, without the loss of innocent life, and without infuriating the Pakistanis for invading their territory. No small order. Obama asked his advisers to present him with multiple possible courses of action for his consideration as soon as possible. If we are to believe the comments from "unidentified sources" close to the situation, every military and intelligence group wanted to be in on the action. Getting bin Laden had been an unsuccessful ten-year quest, and the military team that actually did the job would be national champions and international heroes.

During the next several weeks, advisers presented their proposals, which included bombing the compound with B-2 stealth bombers, deploying drones to fire missiles, conducting joint operations with Pakistani intelligence operatives, and carrying out a commando raid using Navy SEALs. Advisers made their arguments as to why their plan was the best course of action. Disagreements flared up as the operations team discussed the pros and cons of each proposal multiple times. Ultimately, the president decided on the commando raid, and on May 1, 2011, Navy SEALs killed the world's most wanted man.

Even the most serious decisions that executives make come nowhere near the gravity of Obama's dilemma and final course of action. Obviously, the situation was highly unusual, but we can learn a lot from the process. At first glance, the title of this chapter may seem bizarre: leading by *dissent*? But that is exactly what Obama did. He did not want yes-people meeting in advance and presenting him with the single option they thought he would most want to hear. Rather, each group came in with its best ideas, defended them, likely pointed out the flaws in other options, and then let the leader decide. "Of course," you say, "that's how all important decision making should be done." Really? You would be surprised how often leaders surround themselves with sycophants, even though they *believe* they have hired people who will speak their own mind and not hesitate to challenge the boss's ideas. Why is that?

Humans do not deal well with conflict. Even though we give lip service to the notion that we are comfortable with competing ideas, many of us go to great lengths to avoid a confrontation with another person. This aversion probably stems from our ancestors' experiences. Because language was limited, confrontation among cave dwellers often turned physical, resulting in exile, injury, or death—all undesirable outcomes. Remember that the brain's main function is to keep its host alive and safe by avoiding harm. At the same time, our emotional brain is sensitive to our social standing in a group, and it views disagreements as a lowering of our self-esteem, triggering the release of cortisol and the fight-or-flight response. It is far less demanding for the brain to avoid conflict than to confront it.

Although most humans try to stay away from conflict, females are usually better at it than males. There are biological and evolutionary reasons for this difference. Men have a larger amygdala than women do. Recall that the amygdala responds to emotional stimuli and generates emotional responses, such as fear, anger, and aggression. In addition to the smaller amygdala, women have more neural circuits for controlling these emotions. This delayed response came in handy for our cave ancestors; a woman's aggression could result in the loss of her male partner's protection—a perilous situation, indeed. By holding back her anger, the female avoided retaliation from men, thereby ensuring a more stable home environment for herself and her offspring. In the modern workplace, one way to avoid conflict is to surround ourselves with people who think like us. We are generally comfortable with colleagues who have the same perspective on life and whose worldview and thinking style are similar to our own.

Any organization whose leaders all think alike will run smoothly, but it will seldom advance. More likely, the organization will decline.

Organizations are dynamic entities that follow their own version of the law of entropy. Simply stated, *entropy* is the tendency of a system containing more energy than its surroundings to dissipate that energy to its environment. For example, a cup of hot coffee contains more heat energy than the air surrounding it. Heat energy moves from the particles in the coffee and cup to the nearby air particles. Eventually, the coffee, cup, and surrounding air will reach the same temperature, and the particles in the coffee will have far less energy than before. The only way you can get that coffee back up to your preferred drinking temperature is to add energy back into it, by microwaving it or reheating it on the stove. The analogy holds for an organization: its particles are its workers. Left alone in an unchallenging environment, the workers lose energy by becoming complacent and by settling into routine operations. Organizational energy dissipates so slowly that no one notices. Innovation, creativity, and challenge disperse into the environment, and the organization becomes a victim of its own success and, eventually, its competitors.

A classic example of how organizational entropy can affect a company's progress is Dell Computer Corporation. Founded in 1984 by Michael Dell, it grew at a remarkable rate. By 1992, it was on *Fortune* magazine's list of the world's 500 largest companies. It continued to grow rapidly, surpassing the output of other computer makers. It was so successful that Michael Dell stepped aside as CEO in 2004. He thought everything was running well. Uh-oh—that is the first sign of entropy: things are running well! But something else was also happening. Executives were so pleased with Dell's significant market share and success that they thought they could ignore one critical component: customer support. The quality of customer support dropped dramatically because there was so little supervision of it. Despite growing sales, the company's good reputation was slowly dissipating as news of its disappointing customer service spread across the Internet. Although earnings grew by 52 percent in 2005, complaints about Dell's customer service grew 100 percent. Finally, in 2006, Dell executives acknowledged there were problems with customer service and pledged $150 million to fix it. But the public was already disillusioned, and Dell began to rapidly lose market share to Hewlett-Packard. This downturn prompted Michael Dell to return as CEO in 2007, and he immediately focused on upgrading the company's technical support and customer service.

What? You Don't Agree With Me?

Despite his overbearing nature, Napoleon Bonaparte encouraged his senior staff to express their opinions. He wrote, "The people to fear are not those who disagree with you, but those who disagree with you and are too cowardly to let you know."

You need to welcome dissenting voices because they can save a company from the enervating effects of entropy. These voices provide the new energy needed to "reheat" the organization and generate the discussions that challenge the status quo and lead to creative ideas that advance product development. The task facing creative leaders is to find those disparate voices. One way of doing this is to assess the thinking preferences of the leadership teams by using a validated diagnostic instrument. Such an instrument is far more reliable and thorough than the subjective impressions of even the most observant of leaders. Many of these tools are commercially available, and you can find them on the Internet. They offer the leadership team a valuable opportunity to discuss members' thinking preferences. It is important, however, to remember the following about thinking and work style preferences:

- Preferences are neither good nor bad but are assets or liabilities, depending on the situation. For example, a leader with a strong stability force (one of the cognitive forces for decision making discussed in chapter 4) could be a hindrance to an established company contemplating new markets but a godsend to a young company trying to achieve too many goals at once.

- Distinctive thinking preferences emerge early in life and tend to remain stable through the years. Most of us tend to seek out jobs whose work requirements are most compatible with our mind style. We can expand our repertoire of preferences so that we can act outside our preferred style, but it is difficult. It is known as *stretching*. Like a rubber band, you can stretch your mind style, and it will return to its original shape. Stretch the rubber band past its limit, and it breaks. Similarly, people in jobs requiring skills vastly different from their natural preferences feel extreme stress—and sometimes break.

- Understanding the mind preferences of others may make communication and collaboration easier and less combative.

When individuals on your leadership team identify their thinking preferences, they gain insight into how their preferences unconsciously guide the way they behave, lead, and communicate with others. Their actions may encourage or stifle desirable behaviors in their coworkers. When working in a group, for instance, a logical-analytical leader who reveals a step-by-step suggestion for solving a problem will probably suppress the flow of creative ideas from holistic thinkers. On the other hand, a holistic leader whose meetings lack structure in order to encourage openness and creative thought may unsettle those logical thinkers who need time to process ideas and search for logical solutions. In both cases, the leaders are inadvertently stifling the very creativity they seek in others. It is equally important for the holistic leader to recognize the contributions of the logical thinkers as it is for the latter to acknowledge the ideas of the visionaries.

Embracing Different Thinkers

Once you have gained an understanding of your thinking preferences, you should hire and interact regularly with people whose thinking preferences are quite different from your own. This is no easy task; your natural tendency is to prefer to be around those who think and act as you do, thereby raising your comfort level. When you discuss a problem with people who think like you, they are apt to agree with your position and not offer any out-of-the-box ideas that differ radically from that view. Although this validation strokes your ego, no new ideas come into the mix for consideration.

Suppose, on the other hand, you discuss the problem with people whose thought patterns are different from your own. It may be difficult at first to get past the widely varying perspectives. But their feedback is likely to reveal new options that will improve the quality of your decision making. These individuals often offer ideas that complement your weaknesses and exploit your strengths. You will make better decisions when you are forced to look at all sides of an issue and entertain potential solutions that your own thinking preferences might have otherwise rejected.

When trying to talk others into action, you should tailor your mode of delivery to that of the listener. Some people respond better to holistic graphic presentations, while others prefer stories and anecdotes. Logical thinkers get their information by digesting statistics and facts. The point here is to use the thinking and learning preference of the recipient—rather than your own—to ensure meaningful and accurate communication.

Creating Teams in the Workplace

Executives in an organization often start out in a collegial atmosphere. However, if each executive's productivity and compensation are measured primarily in sales, billable hours, and fees, the work environment can soon turn negative. Competition, conflict, and insecurity emerge, producing a stressful workplace that undermines the organization's mission and effectiveness. One way to avoid this negative result is to form teams that work together on a particular case or project. In a workplace with few members, the whole office can be the team. Teams can make important contributions in transforming an organization's culture, implementing change, or generating a fresh approach to an age-old problem. Take, for example, the challenges faced in adapting older marketing schemes developed for one technology, such as radio or television, to the Internet.

When creating teams, remember to avoid homogeneity of thought. Although homogeneous teams will function efficiently, the number of proposed solutions or creative opportunities will be limited. With a broad range of thinking preferences, people cross-fertilize ideas, thereby providing a range of potential and innovative solutions.

Getting team members to acknowledge their differences can be difficult, so you may have to devise guidelines. Establishing rules about how to work together can seem silly to an adult group of professionals whose members might have had years of experience dealing with people. But, in reality, work teams often stagnate because most people tend to value politeness over truth, avoid emotional topics, and opt out of discussions if their proposals are not appreciated. Conflict arises because people who do not understand the cognitive perspectives of others get irritated. Disagreements can become personal. In such a situation, you should depersonalize the conflict and defuse the anger by noting that differences of opinion do not indicate stubbornness but merely represent another perspective. No one thinking preference is inherently better than any other. Rather, each preference brings a uniquely valuable perspective to the discussion, allowing all team members to assess a variety of options and solutions.

Effective Teams

Highly trained executives recognize that they possess specialized knowledge and skills. This mindset prompts them to closely protect their autonomy, especially if promotions and compensation are based on individual performance. Although they may recognize the value of team input, they seldom are willing to make the individual concessions that are sometimes necessary for the good of the whole organization. To ensure that your teams function effectively, consider the following checklist of strategies when forming teams in the workplace:

- Include members who have the expertise to contribute positively to the team's mission. Because cohesiveness is so crucial to success, including a member who refuses to reach consensus or who attacks others personally can undermine or hamper the team's work.

- Make sure the mission is clear. Every member should be able to answer the question, Why am I here?

- Consider hiring a professional consultant to train members in how teams should work. Part of the culture of a team includes discussing the structure of their process and work. This training can enhance communication skills, as well as show the team how to reach consensus, respect the opinions of others, and advocate their decisions to other constituencies.

- Encourage the team to

    + Understand their roles and responsibilities (it is wise to have a facilitator or team leader, a recorder, and one who observes and gives feedback on group processing)

    + Establish ground rules for its operation, such as having a specific agenda, sticking to start and end times, and requiring serious efforts to eliminate interruptions during the meeting

    + Adopt a mechanism for resolving differences of opinion, such as finding a compromise, imposing majority rule, or tabling the issue for later discussion

    + Formulate a strategy for dealing with personal conflicts that arise during the team's meeting, such as one person dominating the discussion or blocking decision making

    + Adopt measures that periodically monitor the team's progress toward its goals

    + Ensure that outcomes and deadlines are clearly explained

How Teams Fail

Teams are likely to fail when the members do not clearly understand the team's mission, fail to buy into the team's purpose or goals, and do not understand or carry out their roles and responsibilities. Sometimes team members do not realize the processes needed to work as a team, such as building consensus, listening, and accepting the opinions of those they disagree with. Be on the lookout for these warning signs and act accordingly.

Controlling Stress in the Workplace

There are leaders who resist embracing different thinkers in their decision-making circles because they believe such an arrangement increases the stress levels of others. Yet everyone is under some degree of pressure in the workplace. Sometimes external pressures are a positive factor, helping people to be more productive, even when faced with controversial ideas. Some people actually thrive under short-term added pressure, and they often say that stress is a good thing because it brings excitement to their work. The human body is designed to meet these temporary demands. Granted, many people who get excited by working hard in a manageable way toward an achievable goal are happy, but they also are not under continuous stress as defined here.

Stress is a health risk, and excessive and prolonged stress can take its toll. Figure 5.1 shows how stress can affect the brain, the body, emotions, and behavior.

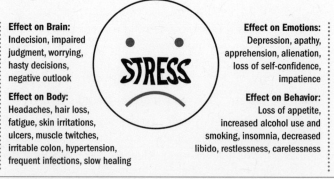

Effect on Brain:
Indecision, impaired judgment, worrying, hasty decisions, negative outlook

Effect on Body:
Headaches, hair loss, fatigue, skin irritations, ulcers, muscle twitches, irritable colon, hypertension, frequent infections, slow healing

Effect on Emotions:
Depression, apathy, apprehension, alienation, loss of self-confidence, impatience

Effect on Behavior:
Loss of appetite, increased alcohol use and smoking, insomnia, decreased libido, restlessness, carelessness

Figure 5.1: There are many effects of constant stress.

When under stress, the body releases extra amounts of a substance called *cortisol*, a steroid that is normally present to regulate glucose metabolism, blood pressure, and immune response. The consistent presence of abnormally large amounts of cortisol in the blood impairs cognitive performance and reasoning abilities; the brain must decide whether you need to flee the situation or stand and fight. Excessive cortisol also impairs memory, raises blood pressure, and decreases bone and tissue formation, leading to deterioration of heart muscle and other organs.

Numerous factors can cause stress, not all of which are work related. Some stress is caused by conditions at home or by personal health problems that are independent of the workplace. Here are some of the common causes of *work-related* stress. Do any of them apply to you? Circle Yes or No.

Long or inflexible hours	Yes	No
Excessive time away from home and family	Yes	No
Confusion about duties and responsibilities	Yes	No
Lack of job security	Yes	No
Conflict among colleagues	Yes	No
Harassment of all types	Yes	No
Lack of control over work; a sense of powerlessness	Yes	No
Excessive time pressures and unreasonable deadlines	Yes	No
Continuous unreasonable demands in performance	Yes	No
Poor attempts at communication and conflict resolution	Yes	No

How did your survey turn out? If you checked five or more causes, you really need to do something quickly to manage your stress. As far as I know, we live this life only once. It already goes by too quickly, and it should not be shortened by an overly stressful job.

Deal With Your Own Stress

Your daily life is likely filled with hectic, disjointed, and tense situations that often require immediate decisions and conflict resolution. Maintaining this frenzied pace takes a toll on your mental equilibrium, upsetting the delicate balance of compassion, ethics, and justice that you need to make sound decisions. Here are a few suggestions to restore your focus and sense of inner balance:

- **Start your day off peacefully**. Use silence, soothing music, reflection, or meditation to start your day. Normal cortisol levels tend to be significantly higher in the early morning, so getting a relaxed start to the day keeps these levels under control.

- **Create your own measures of personal change**. Create personal measures you can use to determine whether you are becoming a better person and colleague. These measures help you evaluate positive changes in your behavior, such as getting angry less or becoming more patient.

- **Slow things down**. If a group or meeting is moving too fast, slow yourself down by sitting back, reflecting, and taking a deep breath. If you are conducting the meeting, slow the group down as well. If someone requests an answer from you, smile first and speak softly. Demonstrating some patience here can go a long way in lowering everyone's stress levels.

- **Practice gratefulness**. Find the time to count your blessings and be grateful for what you have. Expressing your gratefulness to colleagues can improve professional relationships dramatically.

- **Expect surprise**. Accept surprise as a fact of life, and do not get thrown by it.

- **Take time to exercise**. When under stress, find time to stretch and go for a walk. Physical exercise brings more oxygenated blood to the brain, stoking your decision-making processes. Vigorous exercise burns up adrenaline and releases pleasure-producing chemicals called endorphins, thereby lowering your stress level.

- **Talk to others**. Confiding in trusted friends or relatives is a useful way to articulate worries and negative feelings. It can give you a fresh perspective and help make stressful situations more manageable.

- **Learn to be mindful**. Mindfulness means avoiding an instant response to a situation and giving yourself time to determine all the options you have available before acting.

- **Watch your diet**. People under stress often avoid eating, making them even more susceptible to stress factors. Eat and drink healthfully. Vitamin C is important because it helps maintain the immune system, which is often compromised during periods of high stress. Avoid excessive alcohol, tobacco, and caffeine, all of which increase stress levels.

- **Maintain a life outside work**. Be sure you get involved in activities outside work that help you to meet new people. Find ways to have fun by starting a creative hobby that takes your mind away from work worries and reminds you that there is more to life than the office.

In most organizations, stress is an inevitable companion. To some degree, that is desirable. Without challenges and pressures, work lacks excitement and meaning. But we all have the capacity to be overwhelmed by work-related stress and to experience its exhausting and unhealthy effects. Do not let that happen to you.

Deal With Stress in Others

If you recognize stress in a colleague, do something about it—especially if you are that person's supervisor. If you cannot handle the situation, identify someone who can. Later, discuss with the colleague the work-related factors that caused the stress and then determine what you can do to moderate those factors. Do not assume the situation will automatically improve or hope the colleague will become more resilient. Because the continuing presence of cortisol in the bloodstream undermines emotional stability, it is more likely that things will get worse. If you cannot eliminate the cause of the colleague's stress, consider removing the person from the situation causing the stress. Share the techniques you use to deal with your own stress and, if needed, suggest appropriate counseling.

Remember to Laugh

Author and editor Norman Cousins suffered from severe inflammatory arthritis for years.[1] In his book, he describes how just ten minutes of laughter from watching clips of Marx Brothers' movies seemed to lessen the inflammation as well as the pain. In fact, this self-prescribed therapy was so effective that he was able to return to work at the University of California, Los Angeles Medical School to investigate how emotions affect health. It turns out there was merit to Cousins' therapy. Several clinical studies have shown that patients who watched humorous movies needed less painkilling medicine following surgery than those who watched serious films or none at all.[2]

Humor has many benefits when used frequently and appropriately in the workplace and in other settings. Self-deprecating humor is always a hit. Colleagues like to see your human side and hear about your own quirks. Perhaps you are not a jokester, but you can at least encourage others to laugh and ensure that the workplace puts people at ease so they can be their most productive. For the skeptics, here are some of the physiological and psychological benefits of using humor:

- **Releases more oxygen into the bloodstream**. You know that the brain needs oxygen for fuel. When you laugh, you get more oxygen in the bloodstream, so the brain is better fueled. That means you are likely to use your thought processes more effectively.

- **Causes endorphins to surge**. Laughter causes the release of endorphins into the bloodstream. Endorphins are the body's natural painkillers, and they also give you a feeling of euphoria. In other words, you enjoy the moment in body as well as in mind. Endorphins counteract the negative effects of cortisol that may be present because of stress. Furthermore, endorphins also stimulate the brain's memory systems, so you are more likely to remember what you are mentally processing (and learning) while laughing.

- **Provides other physiological benefits**. Laughter reduces your blood pressure, stimulates the immune system, and relaxes tense muscles.

- **Gets attention**. The first thing you have to do when starting a meeting is get the listener to focus. Because the normal human brain loves to laugh, starting with a humorous tale (such as a joke, pun, or story) gets attention. Humor should not be limited to an opening joke or story. Because of its value as an attention-getter and retention strategy, it is wise to look for ways to use humor periodically within the context of your agenda.

- **Creates a positive climate**. When people laugh together, they bond and a community spirit emerges—all positive forces for a climate conducive to working together and learning.

- **Increases retention**. Emotions enhance memory, so the positive feelings that result from laughter increase the probability that the listeners will remember what they learned.

- **Improves everyone's mental health**. Workers in dynamic organizations are under more stress than ever. Taking time to laugh can relieve that stress and give staff members a better mental attitude with which to accomplish their tasks. Adopt this rule: we take our work seriously but ourselves lightly.

- **Acts as an effective management tool**. Good-natured humor (not teasing or sarcasm) can be an effective way for you to remind employees and colleagues of their responsibilities without raising tension in the workplace. Leaders who use appropriate humor are more likeable, and fellow workers have a more positive feeling toward them. Furthermore, they set an example by showing that appropriate humor and laughter are acceptable. Laughter adds life to your years and years to your life.

Avoid Sarcasm

All of the wonderful benefits mentioned are the result of using wholesome humor that everyone can enjoy, rather than sarcasm aimed at a colleague, which is inevitably destructive to someone. Sarcasm comes from the ancient Greek word *sarkazein*, which literally means "to strip off flesh." A person using sarcasm reveals contempt and insensitivity and reinforces stereotypes by singling out a particular person or group. Even some well-intentioned leaders say, "Oh, I know my colleagues very well, so they can take sarcasm. They know I'm only kidding." That line of reasoning led Victorian-era essayist Thomas Carlyle to view sarcasm as "the language of the devil; for which reason, I have long since as good as renounced it." More than ever, today's workplaces are under stress, and people come to their jobs looking for moral and emotional support. Sarcasm undermines that support and turns workers against their peers and the organization.

Being Humble

One of the major reasons you invite dissent into the decision-making process is to remind your colleagues that you do not have all the answers. That realization may not sit easily with some executives who believe that their coworkers expect them to know everything or that humility interferes with success. Not true. Coworkers are well aware that you are human, that you could not have possibly experienced everything there is to experience, and that you will make mistakes, as we all do. Competitive markets are changing much too quickly for any one executive to keep up with all the new trends and emerging technologies. Demonstrating genuine humility tells colleagues that you know your limitations and that you want and value their contributions.

Acting with humility does not call for you to be meek, and it does not, in any way, lower your own self-worth. Instead, it tells others that you are willing to listen to their feedback. Notice the reference to "genuine humility." That means you establish a personal demeanor and a work environment in which coworkers and clients feel safe expressing opinions and offering suggestions that may vary considerably from your own. Someone might actually have a better idea than you do. Accept this as a form of humility. The greater your humility, the more you are open to the opinions of others, and the more you learn.

Being Confident

Ever notice how company taglines spew confidence? Nike says, "Just do it!" It does not ask, "Why don't you think about it?" McDonald's says, "I'm lovin' it" instead of "I kind of like it." Disneyland proclaims it is "The happiest place on Earth" as opposed to "A good place on Earth." Just as company commercials transmit confidence through their taglines, executives do it through language, belief, and appearance. President Obama's tagline during his 2008 campaign was "Yes, we can!" not "Well, we can try."

As an executive, you have to believe in yourself and convey that belief to your colleagues. Confidence in your abilities will allow you to feel more comfortable listening to dissenting views, and it will have an impact on your ultimate decision. Your brain often bases its decision making on confidence that your decision will stimulate its reward system. When it does, your confidence gets a boost, and future decisions become easier. Trying to be influential without self-confidence is as effective as eating soup with chopsticks. To display confidence, consider the following:

- **Dress sharp**. Our behavior tends to correspond with our clothes. When you dress sharp, you seem sharp.
- **Walk briskly**. Confident people walk quickly and display a sense of purpose.
- **Maintain good posture**. A slumped posture transmits low confidence. Sit and stand up straight, look people in the eyes, and stay alert.
- **Focus on what you have**. Workplace problems can get you down, and your dejection will show in your demeanor. Pausing regularly to reflect on what you have accomplished can give you the motivation to tackle new challenges.

Showing confidence is particularly important in dynamic, fluid, or ambiguous situations. When you sound confident, you sound right, and people are likely to believe you.

A Final Word About Dissent

Although dissent is valuable because it allows different voices to be heard for the good of the organization, too much dissent can be divisive and hinder progress. You can welcome a variety of ideas, but at some point, you need to make a decision and move forward. The dissenters will have to set their notions aside for the good of the organization, just as Obama's advisers did after they presented and defended their ideas about how to get bin Laden. After the president made his decision, dissent ceased, and everyone got on board to carry out his chosen plan.

Decision makers in all organizations often face moral dilemmas and ethical challenges in the workplace. Has that happened to you? What thoughts went through your mind as you pondered the situation? How did you process the information? How did you respond? News reports in recent years have been filled with shocking stories of unethical behavior among business executives—behavior that has brought down Fortune 500 companies and thrown thousands of their employees out of work. What is going on? In the next chapter, you will get some insights into how the brain handles and processes ethical challenges. You will learn what processes lead to ethical behavior and which do not. In some cases, it is not a pretty picture.

Walking to a Better Decision

Sitting slows your thinking. When you sit for more than thirty minutes, the blood in your body begins to pool in two places: your feet and your seat. Blood that is pooled is not doing your brain any good. Once you get up and start walking, your calf muscles alternately contract and relax, breaking up these pools. In less than a minute of walking, you will have about 15 percent more blood in the brain. That means 15 percent more oxygen and glucose, which increases the brain's fuel supply and efficiency. If you have to ask important questions, persuade a dissenter, or make a serious decision, do not remain seated. Above all, do not sit with your feet up on the desk, because in that position, the blood is flowing to the part of your body that should not be making the decision. Instead, get up and move around while thinking through your decision. Get yourself a cordless telephone so you can pace while talking, increasing the likelihood that you will make a better decision. You think better on your feet than on your seat!

CHAPTER SIX

Moral and Ethical Leadership

I look for three things in a new hire: energy, creativity, and integrity. But if you don't get the last thing, the first two will kill you.

WARREN BUFFETT

IN 2001, ENRON EMPLOYED APPROXIMATELY 22,000 PEOPLE AND WAS one of the world's leading electricity, natural gas, communications, and pulp and paper companies, with reported revenues of nearly $101 billion in 2000. *Fortune* magazine named Enron "America's Most Innovative Company" for six consecutive years, praising its benefits for workers and its effective management style. Kenneth Lay was its CEO and chairman from 1985 until his resignation on January 23, 2002, except for a few months in 2000 when he was chairman and Jeffrey Skilling was CEO. Lay was one of America's highest-paid CEOs at the time, earning a $42.4 million compensation package in 1999. He was so successful at the helm of Enron and so respected by his colleagues that, in December 2000, Lay was mentioned as a possible candidate for President Bush's Treasury secretary. Then, something went terribly wrong. In the spring of 2001, word got out that Enron's impressive assets and extraordinary profits were inflated or fraudulent. Numerous unprofitable entities were located offshore and were completely off the company's books. Enron's losses were mounting.

In their detailed account of Enron's rise and fall, authors Bethany McLean and Peter Elkind contend that Ken Lay enjoyed the trappings of being CEO but often ducked his responsibilities.[1] His inaction allowed his greedy associates to make risky investment decisions that were not only immoral and unethical, but also illegal. Nonetheless, Lay knew of the hidden losses. When the stock hit $90 per share in August 2000, Enron executives began selling their shares. A year later, the share price had fallen to $45. Lay sold over $70 million of his stock in 2001 while publicly telling Enron's employees and stockholders to buy more shares because their value would soon rebound and reach the $130–140 range. On November 28, 2001, news of Enron's immense losses became public, and the stock price plummeted to pennies. Not only did more than 20,000 workers lose their jobs, many also lost their life savings and pension funds, which they had invested in shares of Enron, reassured by Lay's calm demeanor and insistence that all was well. Lay was eventually indicted and convicted of fraud, but he died before he was sentenced.

A year later, in 2002, auditors uncovered a $3.8 billion fraud at WorldCom, which was, for a few years, the second-largest long-distance phone company in the United States. The company's CEO, billionaire Bernard Ebbers, had been underreporting expenses and overstating revenues. By 2003, he had inflated WorldCom's total assets by about $11 billion. After emerging from bankruptcy in 2004, bondholders got about thirty-six cents on the dollar, but the common stock was worthless. Ebbers was sentenced to twenty-five years in prison.

Not to be outdone by Ebbers' mere $3.8 billion fraud, Mark and Andrew Madoff, sons of Bernard Madoff, a respected financial adviser and former chairman of NASDAQ, made an announcement on the morning of December 10, 2008, that brought more than an early winter chill to Wall Street. They told authorities that their father had made a confession. His thirty-year-old, highly successful asset management firm, with accounts valued at $65 billion, was an elaborate and massive Ponzi scheme. The news hit financial centers like an earthquake. In addition to many individual investors, institutions that had invested in Madoff's firm were also affected. Jewish federations, hospitals, and foundations lost millions of dollars, forcing some to close or temporarily cease operations. Several universities saw their endowment funds plunge. We may never learn exactly how many people knew of his deception. There were rumors for years that something was amiss, mainly because of the overly impressive paper profits he was paying his clients. However, several investigations by the US Securities and Exchange Commission had uncovered nothing illegal. After discounting fabricated gains in value, the actual loss to investors was estimated to be $18 billion. In June 2009, Madoff, at age seventy-one, was sentenced to the lawful maximum of 150 years in prison.

In the meantime, Wall Street was dealing with other scandals that nearly brought the US banking system to a halt. As a result of approving thousands of home mortgages to unqualified buyers, easy credit, subprime lending, and a shortfall of liquidity, large financial institutions, such as Washington Mutual Bank, collapsed. Although some of the home mortgage and equity loans were made in good faith, many were fraudulent in that they violated basic standards for mortgage applications. Underwriters failed to review or ignored the buyers' credit history and sources of income. They accepted inflated appraisals of property and agreed to small down payments from high-risk buyers. No one knows how long it will take the United States to recover fully from the economic recession caused mainly by the immoral and unethical behavior of executives who knew better. Investigators are still trying to answer the question: What happened here? But the more intriguing questions are: Why did it happen? How could intelligent, experienced, and respected executives allow their moral compass to take them so far off course? Surely, greed cannot be the only answer. Did something go wrong in their brains, causing them to perpetrate a fraud that damaged the lives of so many people?

Is Morality Innate?

In previous chapters, we have noted that the brain is a tireless—though not perfect—decision maker. As a young, rational species on the ancient savanna, our ancestors made plenty of personal decisions that affected only themselves, such as what weapon to carry, what food to eat, or what body coverings to wear. Brain networks evolved to help us make such decisions efficiently. However, as we gathered in tribes and interacted with others, social and moral decisions arose and became more frequent. These were very different from personal decisions because they involved and affected other people. The brain had to establish different neural pathways because the brain needed to assess the emotional impact one's decision would have on others. How did the brain accomplish this?

Enter mirror neurons. These specialized neurons do exactly as their name implies: they mirror the actions of others. When you see someone pick up a coffee cup, your mirror neurons activate as though you were picking up the cup. The same happens when you see someone smile or scowl. Researchers now believe that this small cluster of neurons is what helps us to decode the intentions of others and empathize with them through feeling rather than through thinking. You can thank your mirror neurons for the tears you shed when watching a sad movie or the joy you feel watching your child getting married. Studies show that people will donate twice as much money to a charity feeding starving children in Africa when looking at a photograph of a severely malnourished child than when looking at a data sheet showing the millions of starving children in each African country. Our mirror neurons are stirred by the photo of a hungry child, not by a list of numbers.

Numerous research studies have found that individuals with autism have little or no activity in their mirror neuron system. One study, for example, detected no mirror neuron activity when autistic subjects were looking at photographs of the faces of people in various emotional states.[2] They recognized the different facial expressions but were not able to relate them to any particular emotion. This finding helps explain why people with autism have great difficulty interpreting the intentions of others; their mirror neuron system is not functioning normally, probably the result of a genetic defect.

Personal decisions, such as what jar of jam or car to buy, are centered on what will bring you joy. No one else is directly involved, so a selfish decision is OK. Mirror neurons do not need to get involved. Just listen to your unconscious thought processes and choose the option that makes you content. Moral decisions, on the other hand, involve others. Making a selfish decision in these instances runs counter to your genetic makeup and can get you in trouble with your family, community, and even the law.

The emotional brain, then, does possess a moral monitoring system in that it responds to the feelings of others, and its mirror neurons play an important role when you are dealing with moral dilemmas. Assuming no serious developmental problems (such as child abuse) or genetic pathologies, the human mind will develop an innate sense of sympathy for the plight of fellow humans and a desire to care about one another. We are wired to feel the pain of others, and we are distressed if we are the cause of that pain.

The Two Sides of Morality

What are morality and ethics? They are very closely related. Morality relates to understanding the difference between right and wrong. Ethics refers to a code of behavior based on moral principles that guides one to do the right thing. For example, suppose you observe someone in an electronics store shoplifting computer items. Stealing is morally wrong as well as illegal. Your personal ethical code should prompt you to advise the store's security personnel of the thief's actions.

It is not always easy to act ethically. Would you be as willing to notify security if the thief was a poorly dressed woman with a sickly looking infant pocketing a package of baby formula in a supermarket? It is still stealing, but might you hesitate in this instance? What if your son tells you he hit and damaged a parked car and then drove away from the scene without leaving any contact information? That is illegal. Would you call the police? Although moral codes are meant to be free of emotions—think of the dispassionate judge—in reality, emotions are closely tied to moral judgments and ethical behavior.

If you have ever taken a course in psychology or philosophy, you may have been introduced to moral dilemmas—those precarious situations in which you have to make a moral choice of which action to take. The "trolley problem" is one common dilemma used by professors and researchers, and it comes in several versions. In one version, you are standing next to a switch alongside a trolley track and notice that a runaway trolley is about to hit a group of five people who are unaware of their danger. If you switch the track, the trolley will hit only one person. What do you do? Most people say they would switch the track because five lives are worth more than one.

In the second version, you are standing on a bridge over the trolley track and an overweight person is next to you. You are presented with the same scenario: you see that the runaway trolley is traveling toward five unaware people. What do you do? Do you push the overweight person off the bridge and onto the track to stop the trolley? Notice that the moral rationale is the same: sacrifice one life to save five. Surprisingly, in this second version, most people say they would not push the overweight stranger onto the track. Why the different answers to these two versions of the same moral dilemma posed by the trolley problem? Was the brain treating them as separate actions even though the moral justification was the same?

Researchers wondered whether fMRI scans would help them solve this puzzle. Joshua Greene, then a graduate student in psychology at Princeton University, and his colleagues, asked undergraduate students how they would respond to the moral dilemma posed by the

two versions of the trolley problem.[3] At the same time, the researchers were scanning the participants' brains for activity. The results
suggested that because the first version was impersonal and the second version was personal, people engaged different brain areas and
reached two different conclusions. In the first version, cognitive brain
areas associated with abstract reasoning and problem solving showed
increased activity while the participants were considering this impersonal moral dilemma. The information—"I can't really see the other
guy, and I don't know him"—ran straight through their prefrontal
cortex, which coldly balanced costs and benefits and concluded: pull
the switch. However, in the second version, the brain areas associated
with emotion and social cognition exhibited increased activity while
participants were pondering this personal moral dilemma—"He's
standing right next to me and smiling." Those brain regions caused
them to feel empathy for the stranger and hesitate to shove him off
the bridge. Although this fMRI experiment does not tell us the correct
answer to the trolley problem, it does reveal how many of us make
moral decisions. If there is a personal connection to the dilemma,
then the brain regions responsible for emotional and empathetic
response spring into action and guide our response. In the absence of
a personal connection, however, our response is cold and calculating.

Greene, now at Harvard University, has pursued these studies and
argues that the brain is of two minds when it comes to morality. On
the one side, it can be selfish, calculating, and survivalist; on the other,
self-sacrificing, compassionate, and altruistic. Many moral dilemmas
force a choice between two undesirable situations, such as the trolley
problem: kill one or let five die. Our emotional system gets very much
involved when our actions to help some people (throw the overweight
person off the bridge to stop the trolley) will bring harm to others (the
overweight person dies). So is morality wired into the brain? What is
the connection between emotions and moral judgment?

Recent fMRI experiments conducted by Michael Koenigs and
his colleagues, working at Harvard, Caltech, and the University
of Southern California, may have provided some valuable clues to
answer these questions.[4] The researchers tested three groups of people: patients with damage to a brain area just above the eye sockets
(known as the *ventromedial prefrontal cortex*, or VMPFC), patients with
damage to other brain regions, and persons with no neurological
damage. These groups tackled decision-making scenarios containing
different levels of moral conflict. The VMPFC-damaged patients were

much more likely than the other two groups to select practical or utilitarian choices in moral dilemmas—that is, judgments that favor the collective welfare over that of fewer individuals. Apparently, if an aneurysm or a tumor knocks out brain cells in the VMPFC in an individual, everything else may appear normal, but his or her ability to think straight about some issues of right and wrong may become permanently distorted. These patients had injured an area that links emotion to cognition, and the test results underscore the pivotal role played by unconscious empathy and emotion in guiding moral decisions. Without the VMPFC's influence, empathy is set aside and pure reason takes over. In other words, these people will push the person off the bridge to stop the trolley. We noted earlier that the emotional brain and rational brain communicate with each other when dealing with significant problems. In the case of moral dilemmas, it appears that the interactions between the VMPFC in the rational brain and the amygdala in the emotional brain result in moral judgments.

Knowing that a situation is right or wrong (moral code) is one thing; acting in that situation (ethical behavior) is another. In the absence of evidence to the contrary, we have to assume that the VMPFC–amygdala connections in Kenneth Lay, Bernard Ebbers, Bernard Madoff, and other dishonest bankers were in place. Nothing was wrong with their neural circuits responsible for rendering moral decisions. They all knew the difference between right and wrong. But they chose to engage in behavior that was inconsistent with what their social brain was telling them, and they all acted unethically. If their moral networks were intact, then what pushed them, and others like them, to unethical behavior? Most likely, it was greed after all. The Roman philosopher Seneca warned, "For many men, the acquisition of wealth does not end their troubles, it only changes them." Greed tempts many executives, and these guys decided to let their code of ethics be exchanged for profit.

Learning Ethical Behavior Begins at Home

We begin forming our moral code and ethical beliefs at a very early age, largely as a result of our environment. Family, friends, culture, and society all contribute to the system of beliefs that guides our judgments and behavior. There was a time when most children learned about ethical behavior at home and through the practice of their religions. But today, families and churches seem to be having less influence in instilling ethical values in our children. Changing family patterns and the powerful influence of television and other technology have loosened family ties. One result is the widespread decline in ethical standards among our youth. A 2010 Josephson Institute of Ethics survey of 43,000 high school students in public and private school yielded results that do not bode well for our society: "Although 89 percent of the students believe that being a good person is more important than being rich, almost one in three boys and one in four girls admitted stealing from a store within the past year. In addition, 21 percent of students admitted they stole something from a parent or other relative, and 18 percent admitted stealing from a friend."[5] In other words, the moral code of a vast majority of students tells them to be a good person, but the behavior of about 30 percent of them is unethical.

Furthermore, 92 percent of students believe their parents want them to do the right thing, yet more than 80 percent confessed that they lied to a parent about something significant. As for cheating in school, 59 percent admitted cheating on a test during the last year, with 34 percent doing it more than two times. One in three admitted they used the Internet to plagiarize an assignment. As if to prove their point, some students even lied on the survey! Michael Josephson, president of the institute, remarked, "As bad as these numbers are, they appear to be understated. More than one in four students confessed they lied on at least one or two survey questions, which is typically an attempt to conceal misconduct."[6] Institute surveys in previous years have found similar results. These youth—some who have already stolen merchandise and many who have already cheated on tests—are entering our workplaces. They will present a daunting challenge to executives who are sincere in establishing, maintaining, and enforcing an ethical code of conduct for all employees.

Ethical Behavior in the Workplace

The Josephson consultants note that several kinds of temptation exist in the workplace that could undermine a code of ethical conduct. One of the most prevalent is cheating—an act that nearly 60 percent (and probably more) of high school students have already admitted to over the last few years. Computers have probably made cheating considerably worse because more work output can be measured, counted, and objectively evaluated. On the surface, this appears to be a good thing, removing subjectivity and holding employees accountable for their performance. But it also encourages cheating, such as altering data to produce the desired results. Middle-level employees often rationalize this unethical behavior as telling the boss what he wants to hear. For CEOs, it is telling the board of directors and stockholders what they want to hear. This behavior is misleading and deceptive.

When personal integrity and accountability do not prevail in an organization, then all forms of dishonesty escalate and take over. The top executives of an organization are accountable for the culture in which their workers (who have ordinary moral weaknesses) make their decisions, for guaranteeing that all organizational activities are carried out with integrity, and for knowing what is really going on. Enron CEO Kenneth Lay publically proclaimed he was unaware that his underlings were providing him with false data on investments and assets. That argument, however, did not convince the grand jury that eventually indicted him on multiple fraud charges. Executives need to take *purposeful* action to ensure an ethical code of behavior among all workers and to discipline those who violate the code. Maintaining ethical behavior in an organization is no easy task. Too many organizations have reward and promotion systems that focus on short-term results. Under such circumstances, intelligent, long-term decision making becomes nearly impossible. Ethical behavior gets corrupted to fulfill the short-term goals.

How is ethical behavior in organizations faring? The Ethics Resource Center (ERC) in Arlington, Virginia, conducts a survey every two years in an attempt to answer this question.[7] The 2009 survey polled more than 3,000 people, 95 percent from the private sector and 5 percent from the government sector. Here are some of their findings. Forty-nine percent of employees said they witnessed misconduct on the job. Thankfully, this was down from 56 percent in the 2007 survey. As for reporting misconduct, 63 percent said they reported misconduct when they observed it, up from 58 percent in the 2007 survey. Analysts at the ERC make two observations about these survey results. First, the positive results of this study are likely to be temporary, because they reveal an important connection between workplace ethics and the larger economic and business cycle: when times are tough, ethics improve. Second, once the economy improves and business difficulties recede, misconduct is likely to rise. Therefore, executives who do not have a strong ethical culture in place will risk the emergence of long-term business problems.

One of the more disturbing parts of the ERC report was the retribution experienced by 15 percent of the employees who reported ethical misconduct in the organization. Of these employees, 20 percent experienced forms of retribution that were not specifically defined. Here are the percentages of employees reporting different forms of retribution:

- 62 percent—My supervisor or management excluded me from decisions and work activity.
- 60 percent—Other employees gave me the cold shoulder.
- 55 percent—I was verbally abused by my supervisor or someone else in management.
- 48 percent—I almost lost my job.
- 43 percent—I was not given promotions or raises.
- 42 percent—I was verbally abused by other employees.
- 27 percent—I was relocated or reassigned.
- 18 percent—I was demoted.
- 4 percent—I experienced physical harm to my person or property.

What do you think would be the results in your organization? How proactive have you and senior executives been in ensuring that your employees are behaving ethically and are reporting ethical violations without fear of retribution? Conducting an anonymous survey in your organization might reveal the answers to these questions.

Ethical Decision Making in the Workplace

As an executive, you can face some tough moral dilemmas. They often arise without warning on an otherwise normal day and require you to demonstrate moral, ethical, and wise decision making. To do so, you need some guidelines and a framework that provide an opportunity for rational discourse in the face of emotional tensions.

Attributes of Moral Decision Making

Rushworth Kidder, president of the Institute for Global Ethics in Rockport, Maine, suggests that the following four attributes are common to decisions involving ethical questions:[8]

1. The decision is "rooted in core, shared values."
2. The decision "centers on right-versus-right dilemmas rather than on right-versus-wrong temptations."

3. The decision provides "clear, compelling" principles for resolving the problem.

4. The decision is "infused with moral courage."

Let's take a closer look at each of these attributes.

Rooted in Core, Shared Values

Core values are those shared by nearly everyone worldwide and that transcend place and time. Acting as the glue that holds diverse societies together, these five values, according to numerous surveys, are most important: truth, respect, responsibility, fairness, and compassion. Their wide acceptance provides a solid basis for making ethical decisions.

Even a cursory look at Bernie Madoff's Ponzi empire shows that he honored none of these values. He lied about where he was investing his clients' money; he had no respect for their trust in him; he ignored his responsibility to handle their money prudently; he unfairly distributed his few profits; and the only compassion he had was for his wife, whom he showered with expensive gifts.

Right-Versus-Right Dilemmas Rather Than Right-Versus-Wrong Temptations

Right-versus-wrong temptations are common in organizations, such as when employees take office supplies home, abuse sick leave, or pad their expense accounts. In this situation, most people avoid the temptation and choose what is right. The tough dilemmas are those that surface when two morally clear options are placed in a situation where they are mutually exclusive. Kidder identifies four types:[9]

1. **Truth versus loyalty**. Personal integrity and honesty conflict with responsibility, allegiance, and promise-keeping. For example: Do I tell a friend interviewing one of my former employees why we dismissed that employee?

2. **Individual versus community**. The interests of the individual conflict with those of the larger organization. For example: Do I accept a very attractive job offer now, or do I keep my commitment to this organization, which has treated me well, and wait until my contract ends?

3. **Short-term versus long-term**. The important concerns of the present conflict with an investment in the future. For example: Do we distribute substantial bonuses to our employees now, or do we use the money, instead, to establish a permanent presence in an overseas market?

4. **Justice versus mercy**. Fairness conflicts with compassion—a clash between the rational and emotional brains. For example: Do I write a negative evaluation for an employee with a continuing dismal sales record, or do I relent because he is still getting over his divorce, even though that was more than a year ago?

Clear and Compelling Principles for Resolving the Problem

The executive needs to have a resolution plan in mind rather than acting impulsively or not acting at all. The primary question here is: What will be the consequences of this decision, and am I ready to deal with them?

Infused With Moral Courage

Individuals display moral courage by facing challenges that could harm their emotional well-being, self-esteem, or reputation. Nonetheless, they pursue the moral challenge, using the five core values to guide their actions. Moral courage is not the same as physical courage. It means having the courage to be honest, fair, respectful, responsible, and compassionate. With these attributes as a guide, you can now explore some frameworks that may help drive your decision making.

Ethical Frameworks

Several ethical frameworks have evolved for decision making, based essentially on the norms of western culture. Associate professor Mary Trefry and her colleagues at Sacred Heart University in Fairfield, Connecticut, suggest that executives use the following four frameworks in simulation exercises as part of ethical training with their employees:[10]

1. **Utilitarianism**. This approach requires that we always act to produce the greatest good for the greatest number of people. An action is either right or wrong, depending on its consequences. Furthermore, the ends justify the means, and individual motivations are not even considered. People guided by this doctrine always pull the trolley switch, because killing one saves five. An individual's decision or an organization's policy is good if it promotes the general welfare more than any other alternative. Utilitarianism encourages executives to focus on the results of actions or policies, and it is acceptable to sacrifice one person's happiness to serve the greater good.

Questions to ask here are: What do you think will happen if you make this decision? How many people will benefit from this decision compared with other options?

2. **Individual Rights**. With this doctrine, we should never take an action that infringes on another person's basic rights, whether these rights be moral (individual freedom, health, safety, pursuit of happiness), human (freedom of speech and religion, education, and equal job opportunities), or legal (those prescribed by law). Any decision is right or wrong, depending on whether the rights of others are improved, or at least not hindered. People guided by this doctrine would not throw the overweight person off the bridge, because doing so would violate his right to life. A question to ask here is: Would any specific person's rights be impaired or violated by making this decision?

3. **Distributive Justice**. This doctrine states that we should not take an action that harms individuals in need in any way. A decision is either right or wrong, depending on whether the harms and benefits are distributed in a fair and equitable way. Also, people should be treated equally, and all people have equal opportunity in society and in the organization. A basic question here is: If you were in the position of those affected by this decision, is this what you would want, and why?

4. **Integrity/Virtue Ethics**. This doctrine focuses on our character and motivations. It holds that we should not do anything that is dishonest and untruthful. Professionals, such as accountants and attorneys, follow a virtue ethics approach through their code of conduct. Business executives have no such uniform code. Nonetheless, if our emotional brain is telling us that a decision is dishonest, then we should not make it because it would violate our integrity. One important question to ask here is: Is there anything dishonest, illegal, or immoral about this action or decision?

No one framework is ideal for every moral dilemma faced by executives in a dynamic organization. Trefry suggests that executives examine all four approaches when making a major decision that has moral and ethical implications. To encourage this approach, she recommends training sessions in which executives use a moral dilemma that has occurred or could occur in the organization and examine it from all four approaches. Using a matrix similar to the one in figure 6.1 makes the process easier and more thorough. After selecting a scenario representing a moral dilemma, the group discusses the pros and cons of each ethical approach. The discussion will show how the moral principles of the participants coincide with those of the organization—important information for you to have when making critical decisions. Some examples of moral dilemmas you could use in training sessions are:

- An employee claims total credit in a team meeting for an idea that he jointly developed with a colleague who is also at the meeting and who now feels his idea has been stolen. What actions could the colleague take, and what are the consequences of each?

- Your company puts its used office equipment on a table and sells it by bid each month. You see a longtime valued employee who is only two months from retirement slip a used laptop from the table into his briefcase the day before the sale. The company has a strict antitheft policy. What do you do, and why?

- Your boss tells you that a junior member of your management team has been dating his daughter and has just broken up with her, leaving her sad and distraught. He wants you to find a way to fire him. The worker is very competent and a highly valued member of your team. What do you do?

Worksheet for Ethical Frameworks Decision Making			
Scenario: [Write dilemma here.]			
Framework	**Pros**	**Cons**	**Other Arguments**
Utilitarian	Benefits: What are they, and who gets them?	Costs: What are they, and who gets them?	
Individual Rights	Who is respected?	Who is injured?	
Distributive Justice	Fair distribution of costs and benefits. How is this done?	Unfair distribution of costs and benefits. How is this done?	
Integrity/Virtue	Honest or virtuous actions	Dishonest or untruthful actions	

Source: Adapted from Mary Trefry, Jill Woodilla, and Andra Gumbus, "Ready to Use Simulations: Dialogues and Decisions: Moral Dilemmas in the Workplace," Simulation & Gaming 37 (2006): 376–377.

Figure 6.1: Use this matrix for evaluating the ethical impact of decisions.

A Final Word About Morals and Ethics

Organizations are a mix of dynamic and complex individuals whose interactions can cause some people to lapse into unethical behavior. Your job as an executive is to remain vigilant. Remember, it takes a company many years to build a reputation for integrity but only a few minutes to seriously damage it. Surveys show it takes an average of three and one-half years to restore the damaged reputation of a company, if it can be restored at all. Consider the revelation in 2011 that reporters from the top-selling London newspaper, *News of the World*, were phone hacking. The British public tolerated this open secret as long as the tactic revealed drug-using celebrities, dishonest politicians, and philandering film stars. But the tide of public opinion turned dramatically when the reporters hacked into the phone messages of a teenage murder victim and the relatives of slain soldiers and missing children. The disgust and revulsion were so great that owner Rupert Murdoch immediately shut down the 168-year-old weekly paper, putting 200 staffers out of work. There was no way the tabloid's already-questionable reputation could ever be saved.

Ethical behavior is based on your moral code—your sense of right and wrong. It means not only doing what is right, but refusing to do what is wrong. This can be difficult to do, especially in an organization where coworkers are competing against each other for salary, position, and executive rewards. It becomes easy to see coworkers as enemies, to compromise ethics to please an unprincipled superior, to hide the outstanding ideas of coworkers or claim them as your own, and to seek unfair advantages that could bring you a promotion. Resist these temptations. Taking the simpler way out is often easier than doing what is ethical. If you are absolutely, positively sure you know exactly what to do—pause. Give your emotional brain, the mirror neurons, and the input from the rational brain time to communicate with each other. Let their responses percolate before you act. Remember that a little self-doubt gives you the opportunity to examine your options, ask the important questions, and recognize your limitations. It helps also to reflect on the words of Mark Twain: "It is curious—curious that physical courage should be so common in the world, and moral courage so rare." If you always do what is right, you never lose.

Now we need to talk about the importance of taking care of your brain. All of your decision making is only as good as the health of those neurons that transmit and consolidate signals to produce thoughts, ideas, and solutions. Do you know which foods can keep your brain sharp and which can slow it down? Are you aware of how much sleep you *really* need? And how is your memory? Do you feel that it is getting worse as you get older? Apart from the infomercial hype about ginkgo biloba, there really are ways you can improve your memory. To find out all this valuable information about brain health, read the next chapter.

CHAPTER SEVEN

Taking Care of Your Brain

*You know you've got to exercise your
brain just like your muscles.*

WILL ROGERS

Your brain works hard to get you through the day. Have you ever thought about it? Apart from its obvious and vital role in coordinating your movement and internal body functions, the brain also has to simultaneously process an enormous amount of external data that are bombarding your senses every second you are awake. As the brain does its processing, it continually sends summaries of what is going on to your consciousness. It lets you know that the shower water is too cold, the coffee is ready, the cell phone is ringing, you are out of milk, it is time to walk the dog, you should wear the blue jacket today, the clock reads 8:05 already, you are going to be late for work, and to bring an umbrella because it is raining. Whew! And you have been up barely an hour.

The brain's phenomenal ability to handle all this information and to make continuous decisions, both consciously and subconsciously, has been the subject of intense scientific interest in recent years. Researchers have poked, probed, and viewed the living brain from all angles, using highly sophisticated imaging techniques. As a result, they have made fascinating discoveries about how the brain works and what keeps it going. Of particular interest to researchers has been how to keep the brain healthy as we grow older and face the challenges of daily life. You read in chapter 2 about one of the most important discoveries: neuroplasticity. The adult human brain is much more malleable than previously thought, so your behavior, environment, and even your patterns of thinking can cause significant rewiring and reorganization of your neural networks. What you eat and do can significantly improve or impair your brain's efficiency and life span, regardless of your age.

How Well Are You Taking Care of Your Brain?

Now is a good time to review how well you are taking care of your brain. Answer the following questions before you read the subsequent text. As you move through the chapter, see how well your answers compare to what you should be doing to keep your brain healthy.

I park the car away from the office building so I can get in a brisk walk before work.	Yes	Sometimes	No
I use the stairs rather than elevators whenever possible.	Yes	Sometimes	No
I get up from my desk and take a short walk about every thirty minutes when feasible.	Yes	Sometimes	No
I eat a breakfast that contains sugar and protein every morning.	Yes	Sometimes	No
I include at least six eight-ounce glasses of liquids a day in my diet.	Yes	Sometimes	No
I eat at least three servings of fish per week.	Yes	Sometimes	No
I eat at least three servings of dark green vegetables per week.	Yes	Sometimes	No
I exercise regularly for thirty minutes at least three times a week.	Yes	Sometimes	No
I get seven to nine hours of sleep on weekday nights.	Yes	Sometimes	No
I take a fifteen- to twenty-minute power nap at work every day.	Yes	Sometimes	No
I meditate at work for fifteen to twenty minutes every day.	Yes	Sometimes	No
I play video games several times a week.	Yes	Sometimes	No

How did you do? Remember, thanks to neuroplasticity, it is never too late to get your brain into tip-top shape. Read on.

Nourish Your Brain

Keep your brain well nourished throughout the day. Brain cells (like all our body cells) need plenty of oxygen, glucose (a form of sugar), water, and other nutrients to function effectively. What you eat and drink can greatly affect your motivation, mood, and mental performance. Figure 7.1 shows the seven components for feeding and maintaining a healthy brain. Let's take a look at each.

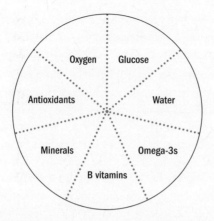

Figure 7.1: There are seven essential components for maintaining a healthy brain.

Oxygen and Glucose

Although the brain represents about 2 percent of your body weight, it consumes about 20 percent of your body's total oxygen consumption and total glucose. Why does it need so much energy? Because it is a remarkable but inefficient processor. When working on a task, it calls on several regions to provide input. Many neurons are firing, and many are misfiring. The brain has to detect the correct signals that are shouting over the noise of the misfires and the stray signals. It is like having ten chefs running around the kitchen to make just one bowl of soup. They waste a lot of energy running about, bumping into each other, and competing for the ingredients.

As a result of this inefficiency, brain cells ravenously consume oxygen and glucose. The more challenging the brain's task, the more fuel it consumes. Take steps to ensure that you have adequate amounts of these fuels present in the brain for optimum functioning, especially if you have a tough mental task ahead. Low amounts of oxygen and glucose in the blood can produce lethargy and sleepiness and dampen mental performance. So, when possible, find ways to keep the blood well oxygenated. Take the stairs instead of the elevator. Park your car farther from the building entrance so you have a greater distance to walk. These little inconveniences pump up your metabolism and increase the amount of much-needed oxygen in your blood. When working on a particularly arduous task, get up from your desk and walk around about every thirty minutes. Take several deep breaths periodically to increase your oxygen levels and alertness. (This deep breathing works best if you breathe in through your nose and out through your mouth.)

Because neurons cannot store glucose, they rely on the bloodstream to deliver a constant supply of this fuel. Do not skip breakfast. Many people do not eat a breakfast that contains sufficient glucose to maintain optimum blood-sugar levels. Eating a moderate portion of food containing glucose (fruits, vegetables, and grains are excellent sources) along with engaging in moderate exercise to increase oxygen levels can boost the performance and accuracy of working memory, attention, and motor function. This becomes particularly important as we get older, because glucose delivery and metabolism slow down, robbing the brain of the fuel it needs for focus, processing, and memory formation. For a quick glucose boost, drink a glass of fruit juice or take a tablespoon of corn syrup or honey. These foods contain glucose that is absorbed directly through the stomach wall into the bloodstream, almost as quickly as if it were injected into the body. Doughnuts and other pastries usually contain dextrose or sucrose. These large sugar molecules are not readily converted to energy and are more likely to be stored, thereby adding weight.

To prepare for a challenging early morning, provide a quick shot of glucose for the brain with oatmeal and brown sugar. If you hate oatmeal, try a banana or a plain bagel. The lack of fat in a bagel allows the body to turn it into glucose quickly. If you have an unexpected meeting that demands brain power, eat some raisins—a rich source of boron. Researchers at the US Department of Agriculture have found that boosting the amount of boron in the body provides an immediate increase (about 10 percent) in attention and memory recall.[1] Apples and nuts are also rich in boron. Consider a cup of caffeinated coffee, because caffeine is a brain stimulant that promotes focus and can help you concentrate. The effects are short term, and you should not overdo it, because excess caffeine can make you jittery. Having a power lunch or working overtime? Start with a glass of fruit juice (instant glucose). Then try a bagel (no fat, slow-release glucose) sandwich of tuna or salmon (omega-3s), and a cup of caffeinated coffee (working memory boost).

Water

Water, also essential for healthy brain activity, is required to move signals through the brain cells. Low concentrations of water diminish the rate and efficiency of these signals. Water keeps the lungs sufficiently moist to allow for the efficient transfer of oxygen into the bloodstream. Make sure that you and your colleagues drink plenty of water. How much water is enough? The long-standing recommendation that everyone should drink eight 8-ounce glasses of water a day is no longer the standard. The current recommended amount is one 8-ounce glass of liquid a day for each 25 pounds of body weight. Thus, a 150-pound person needs about six glasses of liquid per day (150 / 25 = 6). Keep in mind, however, that many other liquids, such as soda, coffee, and iced tea, as well as the water in foods, count toward this total. Both air-conditioning and heating greatly reduce the humidity in your office environment, leading to slow but consistent dehydration. As water evaporates from your body, your blood flow becomes sluggish and your brain signals move slower. Keep water and other liquids nearby. A word of caution: drinking too much water can deplete the body of vital minerals, such as sodium, potassium, and calcium (required for maintaining heart, brain, and muscle function), not to mention the need for frequent trips to the bathroom.

Omega-3 Fatty Acids

Intellectual performance requires certain fats, known as omega-3 fatty acids, in your diet. These fatty acids are commonly found in fish. The body uses omega-3s to make the outer membrane of brain cells through which all nerve signals must pass. Furthermore, as learning and memory create new connections between nerve cells, new membranes must be formed to protect them. Thus, brain cell membranes need a continuous supply of fatty acids. Omega-3 fatty acids lower the risks of stroke and dementia and play a vital role in memory function, especially as we age. Good sources of omega-3s are salmon, tuna, sardine, mackerel, and herring. Vegetarians can use flaxseed oil. Omega-3s are also available in capsule form at nutrition stores. Use these supplements in moderation as high doses may increase the risk of bleeding.

B Vitamins, Including Folic Acid

This group is composed of eight chemically distinct vitamins that often coexist in the same foods. They are essential substances for boosting mood, alertness, and memory as well as improving the brain's resistance to stress. They are important for maintaining healthy skin and muscle tone, as well as your supply of neurotransmitters—those chemicals that move signals from one brain cell to another.

They promote cell growth and division, including that of red blood cells. Many people, unfortunately, do not have a sufficient amount of B vitamins in their diet. B vitamins are all water soluble and thus must be replenished regularly, because any excess is just flushed out of the system. Foods rich in B vitamins and folic acid are whole-grain breads and rice, fish, meat, poultry, fruits, dark-green vegetables, eggs, and milk and other dairy products. Vitamin B complex supplements contain all eight vitamins.

Minerals

These elements play a vital role in many body functions. Calcium (found in milk and dairy products, such as cheese and yogurt) is needed for strong bones, muscles, and teeth. Chromium (found in egg yolks, molasses, and raw onions) helps maintain blood sugar levels and build DNA. Iodine (found in seafood and dairy products) is essential for the proper functioning of the thyroid gland and also helps metabolize excess fat. Iron (found in beef, egg yolks, liver, dark-green leafy vegetables, beans, and bran) is vital for the production of hemoglobin and neurotransmitters. Magnesium (found in whole grains, nuts, beans, and green vegetables) plays a major role in the formation of bones and teeth and in many enzyme reactions. Potassium (found in bananas, carrots, cantaloupe, grapefruit, honeydew, potatoes, meat, and fish) moderates signals that move through and between brain cells and regulates heart function and rhythm. Sodium (found in table salt and many food additives) regulates muscle contractions and maintains the proper balance of water and body fluids.

As for the herbal supplements, such as ginkgo biloba, that claim to stimulate the brain, scientific studies are ongoing but still inconclusive. To date, there is little credible evidence that these supplements actually improve brain functions or memory. If you really want to improve your memory, see the strategies suggested later in this chapter.

Antioxidants

Finally, don't forget the antioxidants. Although cells rely on oxygen for fuel, certain highly reactive forms of oxygen can actually damage brain cells (as well as other body cells). These highly reactive molecules, called free radicals, are produced when your body breaks down food or by exposure to environmental factors, such as tobacco smoke and radiation. Free radicals damage cells faster than the body can repair them. Over time, this kind of radical attack can result in diminished brain function. To offset this attack, the brain needs a constant supply of antioxidants to keep the free radicals under control. This is especially true for older adults because the amount of natural antioxidants in the body decreases as we age. Effective antioxidants include vitamins A, C, and E, as well as beta-carotene, lycopene, and selenium. The antioxidant supply can come from diet or through supplements. However, recent studies indicate that the antioxidants taken in from dietary choices are probably sufficient for good health and that taking supplements showed little added benefits. Antioxidants can be found in fruits and vegetables, grains, nuts, and some meat, poultry, and fish.

Exercise, Exercise, Exercise

The health benefits of regular exercise cannot be overstated. Physical activity increases blood flow and the delivery of nutrients and oxygen to your hardworking brain cells. The frontal lobe seems to benefit considerably from this extra nourishment, resulting in improved executive functions, such as planning, problem solving, organizing, and decision making. Why does this happen? Research studies credit exercise with increasing the levels of *brain-derived neurotrophic factor* (BDNF), a substance that encourages the growth, communication, and survival of brain cells. Imaging studies show that regular exercise increases the flow of blood deep into the brain's memory systems, where BDNF can do its beneficial work. Acting as a kind of fertilizer, BDNF keeps existing neurons healthy, helps them build more communication channels to neighboring neurons, and promotes the formation of new cells.

People who consistently engage in regular exercise outperform couch potatoes of the same age on tests of cognitive abilities. These tests measure attention, reasoning, decision making, problem solving, and long-term memory—tasks that keep an executive sharp and focused. The good news is that even committed couch potatoes can improve their thinking skills if they adopt a moderate and consistent schedule of physical activity. Researchers, such as John Ratey at Harvard and Carl Cotman at the University of California, Irvine, along with their colleagues, report numerous studies showing that regular physical activity at any age improves cognitive functioning and overall brain health in most people.[2] They found that exercise reduces the potential damage to neurons from diabetes, hypertension, and cardiovascular disease. Also accumulating is evidence that exercise may lower the risk for dementia and Alzheimer's disease—potential causes of severe memory loss as we age.[3]

Consider putting a treadmill in your office. Take an exercise break instead of a coffee break. Remember, the exercise does not have to be vigorous, just regular. Human beings are physically and mentally designed to be in motion, and evolution has given us the appendages and cerebral networks to make that happen. Defying this genetic predisposition leads to lethargy and the general deterioration of cognitive, physical, and psychological functions. Don't let that happen to you!

Sleep, Perchance to Dream

When faced with a difficult decision, have you ever said, "Let me sleep on it, and we'll discuss it tomorrow"? "Sleeping on it" can actually help you make good decisions. Although we think of sleep as a time for rest, that is hardly the case with your brain. Amazingly, your brain is about 20 percent more active when you are asleep than when you are awake. That fact alone should convince you of how important sleep is to healthy brain function. Psychiatrist Robert Stickgold at Harvard Medical School and neurologist Jeffrey Ellenbogen at Massachusetts General Hospital are researchers who study sleep and cognition.[4] Figure 7.2 illustrates what their studies show is going on in your brain during sleep.

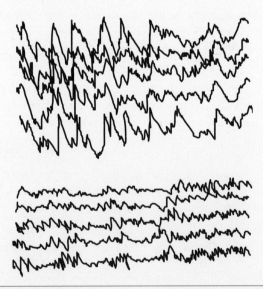

Figure 7.2: The top illustration shows what brain waves look like during some phases of sleep. Note the greater activity in the top illustration compared to the bottom illustration of brain waves during wakefulness.

Their results suggest the following ideas:

- The brain is going through the day's information, sorting, copying, and deciding what to encode into long-term memory.
- Sleep stabilizes your memories and helps them resist interference from other information, so you can recall and use them more easily and accurately the next day.
- Sleep strengthens existing memories.
- If an experience contains both emotional and unemotional components, sleep keeps the emotional elements and lets the unemotional details fade away.
- Sleep can discover relationships among collections of memories and find meaning in what you learned.
- Sleep analyzes new memories, enabling the brain to infer new information and solve problems you were working on while awake.

These research revelations provide ample evidence that sleep is vital for cognitive processing. Length of sleep time is also important; the researchers found that some aspects of memory consolidation occur only after six hours of sleep. If you miss a good night's sleep, you might lose some important memories—maybe even the potential solution to a problem at work.

Sleep loss has become a national epidemic. A 2008 study by the Centers for Disease Control and Prevention found that more than 35 percent of adults between the ages of twenty-five and sixty-five years say they unintentionally fell asleep during the day at least once in the previous month.[5] If that does not get your attention, how about this: 5 percent reported nodding off or falling asleep while driving!

How much sleep do you really need? According to the National Sleep Foundation, the average adult needs from seven to nine hours of sleep each night.[6] The exact amount varies among individuals. To test your ideal sleep time, pay attention to how you feel after different amounts of sleep. Are you alert and productive after seven hours, or does it take closer to nine hours? For better sleep, establish a consistent sleep and wake schedule, avoid caffeine and alcohol close to bedtime, and finish eating at least two to three hours before you retire. To be at your best, make sleep a priority by stopping what you are doing at home as bedtime nears so you get all the sleep you need.

If you do not get sufficient sleep, many of your body's functions are thrown out of whack. Apart from feeling sluggish and irritable, your cognitive skills can be significantly impaired. Researchers William Killgore at Harvard Medical School and Matthew Walker at University of California, Berkeley, have been studying the effects of sleep deprivation.[7] In separate studies, they note that brain images show the prefrontal cortex to be particularly susceptible to inadequate sleep. Apart from the decrease in attention and alertness and the slowing down of response speed, higher-order cognitive processes, such as creativity and innovative and divergent thinking (assessing alternative solutions), are also degraded by sleep loss. Furthermore, sleep deprivation affects cognitive systems that rely on emotional data during processing. This suggests that mirror neurons and the VMPFC system that contribute to social and moral decision making may be impaired because of persistent sleep deprivation. Walker notes that just the loss of one night's sleep can impair the functioning of the hippocampus, which you recall is responsible for encoding new learning into long-term memory. You can avoid all this by enjoying a good night's sleep—every night. It is good for your body and good for your brain.

Once upon a time, falling asleep on the job was grounds for instant dismissal. Now, taking a power nap at the workplace might get you a promotion. Power naps are short (twenty minutes or less) naps taken during the workday. We read earlier that 35 percent of adults said they napped during the day at least once a month. But if they nap at work, they have to do it in secret, probably in the back of their cars during lunchtime. Now research comes to the rescue, confirming that short daytime naps can reduce sleepiness and improve cognitive functioning. Psychologist Nicole Lovato and her colleague at Flinders University in Adelaide, South Australia, have shown that the cognitive benefits of fifteen-minute naps show up immediately after the nap and last from one to three hours and that the benefits from a thirty-minute nap can last for many hours.[8] Early afternoon seems to be the most favorable time for getting the maximum benefits. This is the time of day when cognitive processes normally slow down for most people. Thus, a short nap during this downtime appears to pay off with significant improvements in cognitive performance. Furthermore, a short nap in early afternoon will not interfere with your regular nighttime sleep.

Beethoven, Napoleon, Einstein, Winston Churchill, and Bill Clinton have all admitted to daytime napping to get them through the stress of their work. Companies in North America and other countries are recognizing the value of a short midday nap to their employees. These organizations include British Airways, Google, Nike, Pizza Hut, and Union Pacific Railroad. So, take a power nap and be more alert and productive. If you try it, remember the following:

- Take your nap between 1:00 p.m. and 3:00 p.m., right after lunch.

- Avoid alcohol or caffeinated beverages at lunch as they disrupt the sleep cycle.

- Nap for just fifteen to twenty minutes to avoid getting into a deep sleep and feeling sluggish when you awaken.

- Turn off your phone and email.

- If necessary, use noise-canceling headphones and an eyeshade to diminish environmental distractions.

Boost Your Brain Power

There is little argument that regular exercise, good nutrition, adequate sleep, and avoiding stress will keep your brain healthy and help you reach your full potential. However, is it possible for you to *raise* that potential by building a better brain? Can you make yourself smarter by raising your IQ? If so, how do you do it?

You could start on the Internet, which is crammed with suggestions and products for improving your memory and enhancing cognitive processing. Many of them are based on unsubstantiated claims and dubious research, yet people spend a lot of money on these remedies, hoping to find ways to not only stay smart, but also get smarter. Although neuroscience has made incredible advancements in the last twenty years, the search for scientifically valid interventions to improve cognitive function has not been very successful. This is mainly because scientists do not yet fully understand the biological mechanisms that result in enhanced cognitive function—greater intelligence, so to speak. But some clues are definitely emerging.

Numerous animal and human studies show that enhanced cognitive function results when the brain has more neurons, more neuron connections, a steady growth of new neurons, and plenty of that BDNF fertilizer we discussed earlier. All of these improve memory, learning, creativity, and higher-order thinking—indicators of greater intelligence. Furthermore, studies reveal that the brain circuits of people who excel at a certain task are far more efficient in that they use up less energy, even as the cognitive task becomes more difficult. This is because extensive neural networks allow signals to move quickly and connect to those brain regions that can complete the task. So what can you do to increase neuron number and connections, grow new neurons, and keep them healthy with plenty of BDNF? There are three good possibilities that recent reliable research suggests: exercise, meditation, and video games.

Smart Pills?

As scientists learn more about the neural circuits involved in intelligence, it is possible that drugs could be designed for cognitive enhancement. Some drugs could enhance the neurotransmitters that regulate communication between brain regions responsible for higher-order thinking and problem solving. Other drugs could stimulate the growth of new neurons, especially in the prefrontal cortex—the center of executive functions. Although the emergence of IQ pills would seem like a welcomed treatment for those with mental deficits, they raise several ethical and moral questions that are beyond the scope of this book. Intelligence is a vital resource of any civilization. Yet questions about whether and how to manage, prescribe, and control cognitive-enhancement drugs may be one of the major challenges of the not-so-distant future.

Exercise

We have already discussed the value of exercise, and evidence is accumulating that it not only keeps the brain healthy, but actually contributes to the growth of new neurons and neuron connections through the release of BDNF.[9] Enough said. Just do it!

Meditation

Researchers have known for quite some time that meditation can reduce stress, anxiety disorders, and pain as well as treat diabetes, insomnia, depression, asthma, and high blood pressure. The mindfulness we discussed in chapter 3 is a form of meditation. Only recently have researchers put meditators into brain imaging machines to see what is going on during this process. The results have been surprising. Meditation can increase the thickness of the brain's cell layer (cortex), particularly in those areas responsible for attention and sensation. The growth is not so much due to new neurons, but rather to the increase in connections among the neurons already there, the accumulation of more support cells, and the enlargement of blood vessels in that area.[10] Normally, neurons fire at different times. However, during meditation, they fire in synchrony—likely a sign of increased neural efficiency. All of these results are signs of greater intelligence. Consider learning more about meditation. It will not only relieve stress, but may make you smarter at the same time.

Video Games

A surprising 2004 study at Iowa State University on video game use got the attention of neuroscientists. Medical researcher James Rosser and his colleagues conducted a study with surgeons who used laparoscopic surgery.[11] They found that doctors who spent at least three hours a week playing video games made 37 percent fewer errors in laparoscopic surgery and performed the task 27 percent faster than doctors who did not play video games. Subsequent studies confirmed that video games improved mental dexterity, eye-hand coordination, pattern recognition, memory, and depth perception. Tests showed that consistent gamers had better attention spans and information-processing skills than nongamers.

A good portion of the positive cerebral effects of playing video games comes from their increasing levels of difficulty. Successfully completing one level activates your brain's reward circuits, releasing dopamine, which gives you a feeling of elation. That pleasurable response prompts you to proceed to the next level of difficulty, further challenging your reasoning and building the neural circuits.

A Final Word

In writing this book, my hope was not just that you would finish it, but that it would be helpful to you in the difficult task of leading a productive, vibrant, successful, and ethical organization. Few tasks are more rewarding—and few require so much effort. Maintaining the status quo is comfortable and appealing, but it does nothing to keep an organization vigorous and its employees continually expanding their knowledge base and experience. What happens next depends not on me but on your commitment to personal and professional growth. Here are a few final suggestions for next steps:

- Observe your colleagues. Take notes as they work, and make it a point to learn something new about each one. Connect with them. Ask for their input on how to make the organization work well for them. Follow their lead.

- Take your next step. Just as is the case with each of your colleagues, you have a next step that you must take in order to grow toward your maximum potential.

- Set a specific goal for yourself in becoming a more responsive leader. Set a time line for steps in reaching that goal and stick with the plan.

- Think big but start small. Work with your colleagues and ask them to team with you in planning and carrying out the plans that achieve the organization's goals.

- Recognize your limitations, and accomplish specific tasks by teaming up with specialists who may be more knowledgeable or skilled than you.

- Learn together. Share strategies and management plans.

- Troubleshoot together and share success stories.

- Finally, avoid losing sight of the horizon. You can easily get so caught up in the daily routines within an organization that you have little or no time to work on your long-term goals. Always keep your eye on the horizon.

What comes next is up to you.

Notes

Chapter 1. The Curse of Too Much Information

1. Ap Dijksterhuis and Zeger van Olden, "On the Benefits of Thinking Unconsciously: Unconscious Thought Can Increase Post-Choice Satisfaction," *Journal of Experimental Social Psychology* 42 (2006): 627–31.

2. Claude Messner and Michaela Wänke, "Unconscious Information Processing Reduces Information Overload and Increases Product Satisfaction," *Journal of Consumer Psychology* 21 (2011): 9–13.

3. George A. Miller, "The Magical Number Seven, Plus-or-Minus Two: Some Limits on Our Capacity for Processing Information," *Psychological Review* 101 (1956): 343–52.

4. Michael J. Kane and Randall W. Engle, "Working-Memory Capacity and the Control of Attention: The Contributions of Goal Neglect, Response Competition, and Task Set to Stroop Interference," *Journal of Experimental Psychology: General* 132, no. 1 (2003): 47–70.

5. Dijksterhuis and van Olden, "On the Benefits of Thinking Unconsciously," 627–31.

6. Angelika Dimoka et al., "Reducing the Cognitive Overload in Continuous Combinatorial Auctions: Evidence from an fMRI Study" (working paper, Center for Neural Decision Making, Fox School of Business, Temple University, Philadelphia, PA).

7. Gary Giddings, "Humans Versus Computers: Differences in Their Ability to Absorb and Process Information for Business Decision Purposes—And the Implications for the Future," *Business Information Review* 25, no. 1 (2008): 32–39.

8. Eccles. 12:12 (King James Version).

9.   Shalini Misra and Daniel Stokols, "Psychological and
     Health Outcomes of Perceived Information Overload,"
     Environment and Behavior (2011), accessed April 23, 2011, doi:
     10.1177/0013916511404408.

10. David Bawden, *Information Overload (Library and Information
     Briefing Series)* (London: Library and Information
     Technology Centre, South Bank University, 2001).

11. David Bawden and Lyn Robinson, "The Dark Side of
     Information Overload, Anxiety and Other Paradoxes and
     Pathologies," *Journal of Information Science* 35, no. 2 (2009):
     180–91.

12. Barry Schwartz, *The Paradox of Choice: Why More Is Less* (New
     York: Ecco, 2003).

13. Sheena Iyengar, *The Art of Choosing* (Boston: Twelve
     Publishing Group, 2010).

14. Ibid.

15. Maria Sicilia and Salvador Ruiz, "The Effects of the
     Amount of Information on Cognitive Responses in Online
     Purchasing Tasks," *Electronic Commerce Research and Applications*
     9 (2010): 183–91.

16. Paul B. Andreassen, "Explaining the Price–Volume
     Relationship: The Difference Between Price Changes and
     Changing Prices," *Organizational Behavior and Human Decision
     Processes* 41 (1988): 371–89.

17. David Segal, "Day Traders 2.0: Wired, Angry and Loving
     It," *New York Times*, March 27, 2010, accessed October 26,
     2011, www.nytimes.com/2010/03/28/business/28trader
     .html?pagewanted=all.

18. Dijksterhuis and van Olden, "On the Benefits of
     Thinking Unconsciously," 627–31; Messner and Wänke,
     "Unconscious Information Processing," 9–13.

19. Iyengar, *The Art of Choosing*.

20. Schwartz, quoted from lecture given at Swarthmore
     College, January 6, 2006. Audio available at http://media
     .swarthmore.edu/faculty_lectures/?tag=barry-schwartz.

21. Dijksterhuis and van Olden, "On the Benefits of Thinking Unconsciously," 627–31; Messner and Wänke, "Unconscious Information Processing," 9–13; Iyengar, *The Art of Choosing*.

22. Loran F. Nordgren, Maarten W. Bos, and Ap Dijksterhuis, "The Best of Both Worlds: Integrating Conscious and Unconscious Thought Best Solves Complex Decisions," *Journal of Experimental Social Psychology* 47 (2011): 509–11.

Chapter 2. The Myth of Multitasking

1. Torkel Klingberg, *The Overflowing Brain: Information Overload and the Limits of Working Memory* (New York: Oxford University Press, 2009).

2. "Saving Flight 1549," interview with Chesley Sullenberger by Katie Couric, *60 Minutes*, CBS, February 8, 2009, accessed November 25, 2011, www.cbsnews.com/video /watch/?id=5134473n&tag=mncol;lst;9.

3. David L. Strayer, Jason M. Watson, and Frank A. Drews, "Cognitive Distraction While Multitasking in the Automobile," in *The Psychology of Learning and Motivation*, vol. 54, ed. Brian H. Ross (Burlington, VT: Academic Press, 2011), 29–58; Marcel Adam Just, Timothy A. Keller, and Jacquelyn Cynkar, "A Decrease in Brain Activation Associated with Driving When Listening to Someone Speak," *Brain Research* 1205 (2008): 70–80.

4. Katherine Sledge Moore, Clare B. Porter, and Daniel H. Weissman, "Made You Look! Consciously Perceived, Irrelevant Instructional Cues Can Hijack the Attentional Network," *NeuroImage* 46 (2009): 270–79.

5. Glenn Wilson's studies described in *The Guardian*, April 21, 2005. Available at www.guardian.co.uk/technology/2005 /apr/22/money.workandcareers.

6. Karin Foerde, Barbara J. Knowlton, and Russell A. Poldrack, "Modulation of Competing Memory Systems by Distraction," *Proceedings of the National Academy of Sciences USA* 103, no. 31 (2006): 11778–83.

7. Wesley C. Clapp et al., "Deficit in Switching Between Functional Brain Networks Underlies the Impact of Multitasking on Working Memory in Older Adults," *Proceedings of the National Academy of Sciences USA* 108 (2011): 7212–17.

8. Malcolm Gladwell, *Outliers: The Story of Success* (New York: Little, Brown, 2008).

9. Eyal Ophir, Clifford Nass, and Anthony D. Wagner, "Cognitive Control in Media Multitaskers," *Proceedings of the National Academy of Sciences USA* 106 (2009): 15583–87.

10. Ibid.

11. Paul E. Dux et al., "Training Improves Multitasking Performance by Increasing the Speed of Information Processing in Human Prefrontal Cortex," *Neuron* 63 (2009): 127–38.

12. Peter Bregman, "How (and Why) to Stop Multitasking," HBR Blog Network, *Harvard Business Review*, May 20, 2010, accessed August 29, 2011, http://blogs.hbr.org /bregman/2010/05/how-and-why-to-stop-multitaski .html.

Chapter 3. Respecting the Emotional Brain

1. Joseph E. LeDoux, *The Emotional Brain* (New York: Simon & Schuster, 1996).

2. "Neighbor Kills Area Teen Pulling Prank," *Palm Beach Post*, October 26, 2003, page 1A.

3. "Saving Flight 1549," interview with Chesley Sullenberger by Katie Couric, *60 Minutes*, February 8, 2009.

4. Bill Driscoll and Peter Joffre Nye, *Peak Performance Under Pressure* (Bloomington, IN: Triple Nickel Press, in press).

5. James Dyson, "My Favorite Mistake," *Newsweek* 157, no. 23 (2011): 64.

6. Ap Dijksterhuis and Zeger van Olden, "On the Benefits of Thinking Unconsciously: Unconscious Thought Can Increase Post-Choice Satisfaction," *Journal of Experimental Social Psychology* 42 (2006): 627–31.

7. Daniel Goleman, *Emotional Intelligence: Why It Can Matter More Than IQ* (New York: Bantam, 1995).

8. Antoine Bechara et al., "Different Contributions of the Human Amygdala and Ventromedial Prefrontal Cortex to Decision-Making," *Journal of Neuroscience* 19 (1999): 5473–81.

9. John D. Mayer and Peter Salovey, "What Is Emotional Intelligence?" in *Development and Emotional Intelligence: Implications for Educators*, ed. Peter Salovey and David Sluyter (New York: Basic Books, 1997), 3–34.

10. Numerous studies are discussed in the report published by Cary Cherniss, *The Business Case for Emotional Intelligence* (Consortium for Research on Emotional Intelligence in Organizations, 1999), accessed August 20, 2011, www .eiconsortium.org/reports/business_case_for_ei.html.

11. Margaret Chapman, *The Emotional Intelligence Pocketbook* (Hants, UK: Management Pocketbooks, 2001).

12. Ibid.

13. Ibid.

14. Roger Pearman, "The Leading Edge: Using Emotional Intelligence to Enhance Performance," *T+D* 65 (2011): 68–71.

15. Chapman, *The Emotional Intelligence Pocketbook*.

16. Tony Blair, statement delivered on July 7, 2005, and reported by Associated Press on July 8, 2005.

17. Martin E. P. Seligman, "Building Resilience," *Harvard Business Review* (2011, April): 100–106.

18. Clifton Fadiman, ed., *The Little, Brown Book of Anecdotes* (New York: Little, Brown, 1985): 122.

Chapter 4. Improving Your Thinking

1. Michael Arrigo, "Learning Creativity," SlideShare webinar, 1:26:13, posted September 7, 2009, accessed August 29, 2011, www.slideshare.net/mtarrigo/learning-creativity.

2. Elena Karpova, Sara B. Marcketti, and Jessica Barker, "The Efficacy of Teaching Creativity: Assessment of Student

Creative Thinking Before and After Exercises," *Clothing & Textiles Research Journal* 29, no. 1 (2011): 52–66.

3. Faye S. McIntyre, Robert E. Hite, and Mary Kay Rickard, "Individual Characteristics and Creativity in the Marketing Classroom: Exploratory Insights," *Journal of Marketing Education* 25 (2003): 143–49.

Chapter 5. Leading by Dissent

1. Norman Cousins, *Anatomy of an Illness as Perceived by the Patient* (New York: W. W. Norton, 1979)..

2. Rod A. Martin, *The Psychology of Humor: An Integrative Approach* (Burlington, MA: Elsevier Academic Press, 2007).

Chapter 6. Moral and Ethical Leadership

1. Bethany McLean and Peter Elkind, *The Smartest Guys in the Room: The Amazing Rise and Scandalous Fall of Enron* (New York: Penguin, 2003).

2. Mirella Dapretto et al., "Understanding Emotions in Others: Mirror Neuron Dysfunction in Children with Autism Spectrum Disorders," *Nature Neuroscience* 9 (2006, January): 28–30.

3. Joshua D. Greene et al., "An fMRI Investigation of Emotional Management in Moral Judgment," *Science* 293 (2001): 2105–08.

4. Michael Koenigs et al., "Damage to the Prefrontal Cortex Increases Utilitarian Moral Judgments," *Nature* 446 (2007): 908–11.

5. Josephson Institute of Ethics, "The Ethics of American Youth: 2010," posted on February 10, 2011, accessed November 25, 2011, http://charactercounts.org/programs /reportcard/2010/installment02_report-card_honesty -integrity.html.

6. Ibid.

7. Ethics Resource Center, *2009 National Business Ethics Survey: Ethics in a Recession* (Arlington, VA: Author, 2009).

8. Rushworth Kidder and Patricia Born, "Moral Courage in a World of Dilemmas: Ethical Decisions Grow From a Process That Promotes Rational Discourse Against Emotional Tensions," *The School Administrator* (2002, February), accessed January 11, 2012, www.aasa.org/schooladministratorarticle.aspx?id=4148.

9. Rushworth Kidder, *How Good People Make Tough Choices* (New York: Harper, 2009).

10. Mary Trefry, Jill Woodilla, and Andra Gumbus, "Ready to Use Simulations: Dialogues and Decisions: Moral Dilemmas in the Workplace," *Simulation & Gaming* 37 (2006): 357–79.

Chapter 7. Taking Care of Your Brain

1. James G. Penland, "Dietary Boron, Brain Function, and Cognitive Performance," *Environmental Health Perspectives* 102 (1994): 65–72.

2. John J. Ratey and Eric Hagerman, *Spark: The Revolutionary New Science of Exercise and the Brain* (New York: Little, Brown, 2008); Carl W. Cotman, Nicole C. Berchtold, and Lori-Ann Christie, "Exercise Builds Brain Health: Key Roles of Growth Factor Cascades and Inflammation," *Trends in Neuroscience* 30 (2007): 464–72.

3. Ratey and Hagerman, *Spark*.

4. Robert Stickgold and Jeffrey M. Ellenbogen, "Quiet! Sleeping Brain at Work," *Scientific American Mind* 19 (2008): 23–29.

5. Centers for Disease Control and Prevention, "Insufficient Sleep Is a Public Health Epidemic," last modified March 17, 2011, accessed August 29, 2011, www.cdc.gov/Features/dsSleep.

6. National Sleep Foundation, "How Much Sleep Do We Really Need," accessed November 25, 2011, www.sleepfoundation.org/article/how-sleep-works/how-much-sleep-do-we-really-need.

7.   William D. S. Killgore, "Effects of Sleep Deprivation on Cognition," *Progress in Brain Research* 185 (2010): 105–29; Matthew P. Walker, "Cognitive Consequences of Sleep and Sleep Loss," *Sleep Medicine* 9, no. S1 (2008): S29–34.

8.   Nicole Lovato and Leon Lack, "The Effects of Napping on Cognitive Functioning," *Progress in Brain Research* 185 (2010): 155–66.

9.   Ratey and Hagerman, *Spark*.

10. Eileen Luders et al., "The Underlying Anatomical Correlates of Long-Term Meditation: Larger Hippocampal and Frontal Volumes of Gray Matter," *NeuroImage* 45 (2009, April): 672–78; Britta K. Hölzel et al., "Mindfulness Practice Leads to Increases in Regional Brain Gray Matter Density," *Psychiatry Research: Neuroimaging* 191 (2011, January): 36–43.

11. James C. Rosser Jr. et al., "The Impact of Video Games on Training Surgeons in the 21st Century," *Journal of the American Medical Association: Archives of Surgery* 142 (2007): 181–86.

Bibliography

Andreassen, Paul B. "Explaining the Price–Volume Relationship: The Difference Between Price Changes and Changing Prices." *Organizational Behavior and Human Decision Processes* 41 (1988): 371–89.

Arrigo, Michael. "Learning Creativity." SlideShare webinar, 1:26:13. Posted September 7, 2009. Accessed August 29, 2011. www.slideshare.net /mtarrigo/learning-creativity.

Bawden, David. *Information Overload* (Library and Information Briefing Series). London: Library and Information Technology Centre, South Bank University, 2001.

Bawden, David, and Lyn Robinson. "The Dark Side of Information: Overload, Anxiety and Other Paradoxes and Pathologies." *Journal of Information Science* 35, no. 2 (2009): 180–91.

Bechara, Antoine, Hanna Damasio, Antonio R. Damasio, and Gregory P. Lee. "Different Contributions of the Human Amygdala and Ventromedial Prefrontal Cortex to Decision-Making." *Journal of Neuroscience* 19 (1999): 5473–81.

Bregman, Peter. "How (and Why) to Stop Multitasking." *HBR Blog Network.* *Harvard Business Review.* Posted May 20, 2010. Accessed August 29, 2011. http://blogs.hbr.org/bregman/2010/05/how-and-why-to-stop -multitaski.html.

CBS News. "Saving Flight 1549," interview with Chesley Sullenberger by Katie Couric, *60 Minutes*, February 8, 2009. Accessed November 25, 2011. www.cbsnews.com/video/watch/?id=5134473n&tag=mncol;lst;9.

Centers for Disease Control and Prevention. "Insufficient Sleep Is a Public Health Epidemic." Last modified March 17, 2011. Accessed August 29, 2011. www.cdc.gov/Features/dsSleep.

Chapman, Margaret. *The Emotional Intelligence Pocketbook.* Hants, UK: Management Pocketbooks, 2001.

Cherniss, Cary. *The Business Case for Emotional Intelligence.* Consortium for Research on Emotional Intelligence in Organizations, 1999. Accessed August 29, 2011. www.eiconsortium.org/reports/business _case_for_ei.html.

Clapp, Wesley C., Michael T. Rubens, Jasdeep Sabharwal, and Adam
    Gazzaley. "Deficit in Switching Between Functional Brain Networks
    Underlies the Impact of Multitasking on Working Memory in Older
    Adults." *Proceedings of the National Academy of Sciences USA* 108 (2011):
    7212–17.

Cotman, Carl W., Nicole C. Berchtold, and Lori-Ann Christie. "Exercise
    Builds Brain Health: Key Roles of Growth Factor Cascades and
    Inflammation." *Trends in Neuroscience* 30 (2007): 464–72.

Cousins, Norman. *Anatomy of an Illness as Perceived by the Patient.* New York:
    W. W. Norton, 1979.

Dapretto, Mirella, Mari S. Davies, Jennifer H. Pfeifer, Ashley A. Scott,
    Marian Sigman, Susan Y. Bookheimer, and Marco Iacoboni.
    "Understanding Emotions in Others: Mirror Neuron Dysfunction in
    Children with Autism Spectrum Disorders." *Nature Neuroscience* 9 (2006,
    January): 28–30.

Dijksterhuis, Ap, and Zeger van Olden. "On the Benefits of Thinking
    Unconsciously: Unconscious Thought Can Increase Post-Choice
    Satisfaction." *Journal of Experimental Social Psychology* 42 (2006): 627–31.

Dimoka, Angelika, Gediminas Adomavicius, Alok Gupta, and Paul
    A. Pavlou. "Reducing the Cognitive Overload in Continuous
    Combinatorial Auctions: Evidence From an fMRI Study." Working
    paper, Center for Neural Decision Making, Fox School of Business,
    Temple University, Philadelphia, PA.

Driscoll, Bill, and Peter Joffre Nye. *Peak Performance Under Pressure.*
    Bloomington, IN: Triple Nickel Press, in press.

Dux, Paul E., Michael N. Tombu, Stephenie Harrison, Baxter P. Rogers,
    Frank Tong, and René Marois. "Training Improves Multitasking
    Performance by Increasing the Speed of Information Processing in
    Human Prefrontal Cortex." *Neuron* 63 (2009): 127–38.

Dyson, James. "My Favorite Mistake." *Newsweek* 157, no. 23 (2011): 64.

Ethics Resource Center. *2009 National Business Ethics Survey: Ethics in a Recession.*
    Arlington, VA: Author, 2009.

Fadiman, Clifton, ed. *The Little, Brown Book of Anecdotes.* New York: Little,
    Brown, 1985.

Foerde, Karin, Barbara J. Knowlton, and Russell A. Poldrack. "Modulation
    of Competing Memory Systems by Distraction." *Proceedings of the National
    Academy of Sciences USA* 103, no. 31 (2006): 11778–83.

Giddings, Gary. "Humans Versus Computers: Differences in Their Ability to Absorb and Process Information for Business Decision Purposes—And the Implications for the Future." *Business Information Review* 25, no. 1 (2008): 32–39.

Gladwell, Malcolm. *Outliers: The Story of Success*. New York: Little, Brown, 2008.

Goleman, Daniel. *Emotional Intelligence: Why It Can Matter More Than IQ*. New York: Bantam, 1995.

Greene, Joshua D., Brian Sommerville, Leigh E. Nystrom, John M. Darley, and Jonathan D. Cohen. "An fMRI Investigation of Emotional Management in Moral Judgment." *Science* 293 (2001): 2105–08.

Hölzel, Britta K., James Carmody, Mark Vangel, Christina Congleton, Sita M. Yerramsetti, Tim Gard, and Sara W. Lazar. "Mindfulness Practice Leads to Increases in Regional Brain Gray Matter Density." *Psychiatry Research: Neuroimaging* 191 (2011, January): 36–43.

Iyengar, Sheena. *The Art of Choosing*. Boston: Twelve Publishing Group, 2010.

Josephson Institute of Ethics. "The Ethics of American Youth: 2010." Posted February 10, 2011. Accessed November 25, 2011. http://charactercounts.org/programs/reportcard/2010/installment02 _report-card_honesty-integrity.html.

Just, Marcel Adam, Timothy A. Keller, and Jacquelyn Cynkar. "A Decrease in Brain Activation Associated With Driving When Listening to Someone Speak." *Brain Research* 1205 (2008): 70–80.

Kane, Michael J., and Randall W. Engle. "Working-Memory Capacity and the Control of Attention: The Contributions of Goal Neglect, Response Competition, and Task Set to Stroop Interference." *Journal of Experimental Psychology: General* 132, no. 1 (2003): 47–70.

Karpova, Elena, Sara B. Marcketti, and Jessica Barker. "The Efficacy of Teaching Creativity: Assessment of Student Creative Thinking Before and After Exercises." *Clothing & Textiles Research Journal* 29, no. 1 (2011): 52–66.

Kidder, Rushworth. *How Good People Make Tough Choices*. New York: Harper, 2009.

Kidder, Rushworth and Patricia Born. "Moral Courage in a World of Dilemmas: Ethical Decisions Grow From a Process That Promotes Rational Discourse Against Emotional Tensions." *The School Administrator* (2002, February). Accessed January 11, 2012. www.aasa.org /schooladministratorarticle.aspx?id=4148.

Killgore, William D. S. "Effects of Sleep Deprivation on Cognition." *Progress in Brain Research* 185 (2010): 105–29.

Klingberg, Torkel. *The Overflowing Brain: Information Overload and the Limits of Working Memory.* New York: Oxford University Press, 2009.

Koenigs, Michael, Liane Young, Ralph Adolphs, Daniel Tranel, Fiery Cushman, Marc Hauser, and Antonio Damasio. "Damage to the Prefrontal Cortex Increases Utilitarian Moral Judgments." *Nature* 446 (2007): 908–11.

Kosfeld, Michael, Markus Heinrichs, Paul J. Zak, Urs Fischbacher, and Ernst Fehr. "Oxytocin Increases Trust in Humans." *Nature* 435 (2005): 673–76.

LeDoux, Joseph E. *The Emotional Brain.* New York: Simon & Schuster, 1996.

Lovato, Nicole, and Leon Lack. "The Effects of Napping on Cognitive Functioning." *Progress in Brain Research* 185 (2010): 155–66.

Luders, Eileen, Arthur W. Toga, Natasha Lepore, and Christian Gaser. "The Underlying Anatomical Correlates of Long-Term Meditation: Larger Hippocampal and Frontal Volumes of Gray Matter." *NeuroImage* 45 (2009, April): 672–78.

Martin, Rod A. *The Psychology of Humor: An Integrative Approach.* Burlington, MA: Elsevier Academic Press, 2007.

Mayer, John D., and Peter Salovey. "What Is Emotional Intelligence?" In *Emotional Development and Emotional Intelligence: Implications for Educators,* edited by Peter Salovey and David Sluyter, 3–34. New York: Basic Books, 1997.

McIntyre, Faye S., Robert E. Hite, and Mary Kay Rickard. "Individual Characteristics and Creativity in the Marketing Classroom: Exploratory Insights." *Journal of Marketing Education* 25 (2003): 143–49.

McLean, Bethany, and Peter Elkind. *The Smartest Guys in the Room: The Amazing Rise and Scandalous Fall of Enron.* New York: Penguin, 2003.

Messner, Claude, and Michaela Wänke. "Unconscious Information Processing Reduces Information Overload and Increases Product Satisfaction." *Journal of Consumer Psychology* 21 (2011): 9–13.

Miller, George A. "The Magical Number Seven, Plus-or-Minus Two: Some Limits on Our Capacity for Processing Information." *Psychological Review* 101 (1956): 343–52.

Misra, Shalini, and Daniel Stokols. "Psychological and Health Outcomes of Perceived Information Overload." *Environment and Behavior* (2011). Accessed April 23, 2011. doi: 10.1177/0013916511404408.

Moore, Katherine Sledge, Clare B. Porter, and Daniel H. Weissman. "Made You Look! Consciously Perceived, Irrelevant Instructional Cues Can Hijack the Attentional Network." *NeuroImage* 46 (2009): 270–79.

Nordgren, Loran F., Maarten W. Bos, and Ap Dijksterhuis. "The Best of Both Worlds: Integrating Conscious and Unconscious Thought Best Solves Complex Decisions." *Journal of Experimental Social Psychology* 47 (2011): 509–11.

Ophir, Eyal, Clifford Nass, and Anthony D. Wagner. "Cognitive Control in Media Multitaskers." *Proceedings of the National Academy of Sciences USA* 106 (2009): 15583–87.

Pearman, Roger. "The Leading Edge: Using Emotional Intelligence to Enhance Performance." *T+D* 65 (2011): 68–71.

Penland, James G. "Dietary Boron, Brain Function, and Cognitive Performance." *Environmental Health Perspectives* 102 (1994): 65–72.

Ratey, John J., and Eric Hagerman. *Spark: The Revolutionary New Science of Exercise and the Brain.* New York: Little, Brown, 2008.

Rosser, James C., Jr., Paul J. Lynch, Laurie Cuddihy, Douglas A. Gentile, Jonathan Klonsky, and Ronald Merrell. "The Impact of Video Games on Training Surgeons in the 21st Century." *Journal of the American Medical Association: Archives of Surgery* 142 (2007): 181–86.

Schwartz, Barry. *The Paradox of Choice: Why More Is Less.* New York: Ecco, 2003.

Segal, David. "Day Traders 2.0: Wired, Angry and Loving It." *New York Times,* March 28, 2010: BU1.

Seligman, Martin E. P. "Building Resilience." *Harvard Business Review* (2011, April): 100–06.

Sicilia, Maria, and Salvador Ruiz. "The Effects of the Amount of Information on Cognitive Responses in Online Purchasing Tasks." *Electronic Commerce Research and Applications* 9 (2010): 183–91.

Stickgold, Robert, and Jeffrey M. Ellenbogen. "Quiet! Sleeping Brain at Work." *Scientific American Mind* 19 (2008): 23–29.

Strayer, David L., Jason M. Watson, and Frank A. Drews. "Cognitive Distraction While Multitasking in the Automobile." In *The Psychology of Learning and Motivation,* vol. 54, edited by Brian H. Ross, 29–58. Burlington, VT: Academic Press, 2011.

Trefry, Mary, Jill Woodilla, and Andra Gumbus. "Ready to Use
    Simulations: Dialogues and Decisions: Moral Dilemmas in the
    Workplace." *Simulation & Gaming* 37 (2006): 357–79.

Walker, Matthew P. "Cognitive Consequences of Sleep and Sleep Loss." *Sleep
    Medicine* 9, no. S1 (2008): S29–S34.

Index

difference between intelligence
and, 71
impediments to, 71–72
strategies for improving, 72–74
crisis/turmoil, handling, 54–56

D

Damasio, A., 46
decision making
attributes of moral, 100–102
creativity, 67
emotional brain and, 7, 42–43
impact of information overload
on, 13–17
purpose, 68
relationships, 68
results, 68
speed of, 70
stability, 67
Dell, M., 77
Dell Computer Corp., 77
Dijksterhuis, A., 4, 7, 20
Dimoka, A., 7
Disneyland, 88
distributive justice, 103
Drewes, M., 40
Driscoll, B., 41
Dux, P., 33
Dyson, J., 43

E

Ebbers, B., 92
ego, creativity and, 72
Einstein, 116
Elkind, P., 91
Ellenbogen, J., 114
emotional brain, 5
attention given, 41–42
battle between rational brain and,
38–41
decision making and, 7, 42–43
emotional intelligence
components of, 47–48

crisis/turmoil, handling, 54–56
emotions and stress, management
of, 50–51
gender differences, 49
habits of people with high,
44–46
intrapersonal versus
interpersonal, 49–54
raising, 48–49
self-awareness, 49–50
self-motivation, 51–52
use of term, 43–44
workplace relationships, 52–54
emotions and stress, management
of, 50–51
empathy, 57–58
Engle, R., 6
Enron, 91–92
entropy, 77
error-related negativity, 42, 43
ethics and morals
attributes of, 100–102
banking/housing scandals, 93
decision-making worksheet, 104
definitions, 94–95
emotions, role of, 93–94
Enron example, 91–92
frameworks, 102–104
learning, 97–98
Madoff scandal, 92–93
moral dilemmas, 95–97, 104
workplace, 98–104
WorldCom example, 92
Ethics Resource Center (ERC), 99
exercise, role of, 89, 113–114, 118
experiences, 70

F

focus, need for, 25–26
Foerde, K., 29
functional magnetic resonance
imaging (fMRI), 7

About the Author

DAVID A. SOUSA, EdD, is an author and international consultant in educational neuroscience and in the applications of brain research to professional practice. His fifteen books inform professionals on ways they can translate current brain research into strategies for improving their work. A member of the Cognitive Neuroscience Society, he has conducted workshops on brain research and science education. He has made presentations across the United States, Canada, Europe, Australia, New Zealand, and Asia.

Dr. Sousa is past president of the National Staff Development Council and has received numerous awards, including the Distinguished Alumni Award and honorary doctorates from Bridgewater (Massachusetts) State University and Gratz College. He has been interviewed by Matt Lauer on NBC's *TODAY* and by National Public Radio about his work with schools using brain research. His books include *How the Brain Learns*, a bestseller now in its fourth edition, and *How the Brain Learns Mathematics*, which was selected by the Independent Book Publishers Association as one of the best professional development books of 2008. In addition, his book *How Brain Science Can Make You a Better Lawyer* was published in 2009 by the American Bar Association. Dr. Sousa has a bachelor of science degree in chemistry from Bridgewater (Massachusetts) State University, a master of arts from Harvard University, and a doctorate from Rutgers University.